BestMasters

Mit **„BestMasters“** zeichnet Springer die besten Masterarbeiten aus, die an renommierten Hochschulen in Deutschland, Österreich und der Schweiz entstanden sind. Die mit Höchstnote ausgezeichneten Arbeiten wurden durch Gutachter zur Veröffentlichung empfohlen und behandeln aktuelle Themen aus unterschiedlichen Fachgebieten der Naturwissenschaften, Psychologie, Technik und Wirtschaftswissenschaften. Die Reihe wendet sich an Praktiker und Wissenschaftler gleichermaßen und soll insbesondere auch Nachwuchswissenschaftlern Orientierung geben.

Springer awards **“BestMasters”** to the best master’s theses which have been completed at renowned Universities in Germany, Austria, and Switzerland. The studies received highest marks and were recommended for publication by supervisors. They address current issues from various fields of research in natural sciences, psychology, technology, and economics. The series addresses practitioners as well as scientists and, in particular, offers guidance for early stage researchers.

More information about this series at https://link.springer.com/bookseries/13198

Moritz Miller

Sprintegration® — An Agile Framework for M&A Integration

Springer Gabler

Moritz Miller
Zurich, Switzerland

This Master Thesis was submitted with the original title "PM for M&A: Project Management Framework for M&A Integration" to the University of Applied Sciences (Hochschule für Technik) Stuttgart as well as the Liverpool John Moores University.

ISSN 2625-3577 ISSN 2625-3615 (electronic)
BestMasters
ISBN 978-3-658-37454-9 ISBN 978-3-658-37455-6 (eBook)
https://doi.org/10.1007/978-3-658-37455-6

Responsible Editor: Marija Kojic
This Springer Gabler imprint is published by the registered company Springer Fachmedien Wiesbaden GmbH part of Springer Nature.
The registered company address is: Abraham-Lincoln-Str. 46, 65189 Wiesbaden, Germany

Acknowledgements

I would like to acknowledge my appreciation and gratitude to all supporters throughout the journey of this dual master programme, especially to my two supervisors Prof. Dr. Dr. Andrej Pustisek (HFT Stuttgart) and Dr. Matthew Tucker (Liverpool John Moore University) for their continuous and inspiring guidance during this final research project.

Furthermore, I would like to thank all research participants for their trust and time and for sharing their valuable insights and experiences as a very important input to the research results.

Finally, I would like to express my gratitude to my wife, my family and my friends, who have continuously supported and motivated me.

Due to this support and guidance, I could complete my master programme and this business consultancy project with many valuable experiences and learnings for my future path.

Moritz Miller

Abstract

The aim of this strategic business consultancy project was the development of an applicable project management framework for sustainably successful M&A integration. Although M&As have been undertaken for many decades throughout all industries, the reported high failure rates of M&A cases, that do not fulfil the original expectations, demonstrate the relevance of this topic and the need to create solutions. The literature is rich regarding the general analysis of failure and success, however, it is shallow regarding applicable systems and project management approaches that would allow the transfer to the specific business context. Therefore, this research aims to answer the following central research question:

How can a project management approach lead to a sustainably successful post-merger integration within an international real estate enterprise?

With a high focus on the applicability of all results, secondary data was critically and systematically reviewed to identify transferable reasons for failure and success and best practice for M&A integration, followed by primary data collection through a multiple case study approach including 55 interviews with internal stakeholders from 12 M&A cases and external experts. The synthesis of findings from secondary and primary data led to the creation of an agile project management framework including the detailed elaboration of roles, routines, methods and tools, which were critically appraised and verified with two focus groups. This framework demonstrates the importance of holistic approaches including functional, operational and cultural integration, embedded in an agile system, which enables all involved stakeholders to deal with the high complexity of M&As as the process of combining two previously separate companies and social systems. Thereby this research facilitates learning from previous cases and the integration of external expertise and theory, to continuously improve and enhance personal and organisational maturity towards sustainably successful M&A integration processes, which contribute to higher strategic objectives.

Contents

Abbreviations

CBA	Cross-Border Acquisition
CDD	Cultural Due Diligence
CU	Corporate Unit
D&S	Drees & Sommer
DD	Due Diligence
DOI	Digital Object Identifier
EI/EQ	Emotional Intelligence, Emotional Quotient
EY	Ernst & Young
Fig	Figure
HARP	Heightening Awareness of Research Philosophy
HBR	Harvard Business Review
HR	Human Resources
IT	Information Technology
KM	Knowledge Management
KPI	Key Performance Indicator
M&A	Mergers and Acquisitions
PM	Project Management
PMBOK	Project Management Body of Knowledge
PMI (1)	Post-Merger Integration
PMI (2)	Project Management Institute
PWC	PricewaterhouseCoopers
Q&A	Questions & Answers
RA	Research Aim
RO1-5	Research Objective 1–5

RQ	Research Question
SWOT	Strengths, Weaknesses, Opportunities, Threats
TQM	Total Quality Management
VUCA	Volatile, Uncertain, Complex, Ambiguous

List of Figures

List of Tables

Introduction 1

This chapter provides an overview of the purpose of this consultancy project by elaborating its context and background, leading to the research question, aim and objectives. It thereby supports the understanding of need and value of the conducted research and its allocation within the business context.

1.1 Background

Since the end of the 19th century, mergers and acquisitions (M&As) have been undertaken by companies for different strategic reasons like extension of portfolios and know-how (Duvall-Dickson et al., 2016; Buschmann, 2019), expansion to new markets (Meckl and Röhrle, 2016) or exploitation of synergies (Fiorentino and Garzella, 2015; Rebner and Yeganeh, 2019), to maintain or increase competitiveness and growth (Hromei, 2013; Brekke et al., 2017). Despite these long-term experiences throughout all industries, a high percentage of more than 50 per cent of M&A activities fails to fulfil the expectations regarding speed, synergies, added value and sustainable growth (Koi-Akrofi, 2016; Venzin et al., 2018; Shi and Wang, 2020).

For Drees & Sommer, a German consultancy company, the current strategy is highly related to mergers and acquisitions, which implies these risks of failure. Therefore, this research examines the current peer-reviewed literature on success and failure criteria and global best practice for M&A and reflects them against company-specific insights through primary research and the development of an applicable framework for successful M&A integration.

M. Miller, *Sprintegration®—An Agile Framework for M&A Integration*, BestMasters, https://doi.org/10.1007/978-3-658-37455-6_1

D&S was founded in Stuttgart in 1970 as an expert company for construction project management. Meanwhile, the company has grown to 3.800 employees in 46 offices worldwide (24 in Germany, 22 international). The services have been further developed from a PM office to the German market leader with a comprehensive service portfolio including project management, engineering, infrastructure and consulting (Fig. 1.1), provided to public and private clients throughout all industry sectors.

Fig. 1.1 Overview Service Portfolio (Drees & Sommer, 2019)

Rapid growth based on profitability and increasing market demand exposes companies to the challenges of defining growth strategies (Bruni-Bossio et al., 2018) and adjusting their structures (Foss and Saebi, 2018; Yu et al., 2020). D&S addressed these challenges in 2018 by implementing a new vision (Fig. 1.2) and internal organisation.

Fig. 1.2 Vision 2025, Leading Slogan (Drees & Sommer, 2018)

The vision contains that D&S is a leading European real estate expert in 2025, driven by innovation and circular economy. This addresses five main strategic elements:

- **Leading:** market leadership expansion from Germany to Europe
- **European:** stronger international focus
- **Real Estate Experts:** comprehensive service portfolio
- **Innovation:** stronger focus on innovation
- **Circular Economy:** stronger focus on sustainability

Especially the goals of European leadership and innovation have since 2018 been increasing the focus on M&A, because the slow organic growth of the existing international locations does not lead to the required size and market position without further investments, and additional service lines are planned. Based on the experience of several national and international acquisitions within the last ten years, D&S has continuously improved the functional integration of smaller companies of up to 80 employees. Nevertheless, the planned international expansion includes cross-border acquisitions (CBA) in larger scale, that expose the organisation to challenges like differences in culture, language, business context and local distance (Erel et al., 2012; Boateng et al., 2019), which are risks for failure if not considered properly (Connaughton et al., 2015; Friedman et al., 2016) and which require a more holistic view, including operational and cultural integration (Gerds and Schewe, 2014).

1.2 Problem Definition and Research Question

This strategic orientation requires to learn from previous M&A cases and expert literature to develop a management framework that addresses the specific challenges of an international consultancy firm and proactively minimises the risks that can lead to failure (Meckl and Röhrle, 2016; Joshi et al., 2020).

As the integrations of M&As fulfil all criteria of a project by being temporary endeavours with unique outcomes (Project Management Institute, 2017), which is confirmed by several scholars seeing M&As as unique, complex and dynamic organisational projects (Engelhardt, 2017; Bergamin and Braun, 2018; Meynerts-Stiller, 2019), project management approaches are required rather than operational business approaches. However, there is little literature on traditional or agile project management for this context (Hurta et al., 2017; Patel, 2019), and existing studies suggest further research on the implementation of PM methods for M&A (Patel, 2012; Steigenberger, 2017).

As succeeding in acquisitions during the coming years is essential for the competitiveness and internationalisation of D&S, the following question is highly relevant:

Research Question:

- *How can a project management approach lead to a sustainably successful post-merger integration within an international real estate enterprise?*

1.3 Research Aim and Objectives

This research aims to develop an applicable framework that can effectively be implemented in future M&A cases to support their successful integration.

Research Aim:

- *To create a project management framework for M&As within an international real estate enterprise*

This research aim is broken down into specific research objectives (Fig. 1.3) that build upon each other (Saunders et al., 2019) and cover the analysis of primary and secondary data within the timeframe (Easterby-Smith et al., 2018).

Research Objectives:

1. *To systematically identify and synthesise success factors and failure criteria for M&A in literature*
2. *To critically analyse M&A best practice in theory and practice, with focus on integration management and its prerequisites*
3. *To comprehensively investigate 12 M&A cases at D&S regarding context and lessons learned*
4. *To design and develop a project management framework for M&A integration including applicable methods and tools*
5. *To critically appraise and verify the project management framework in two focus groups*

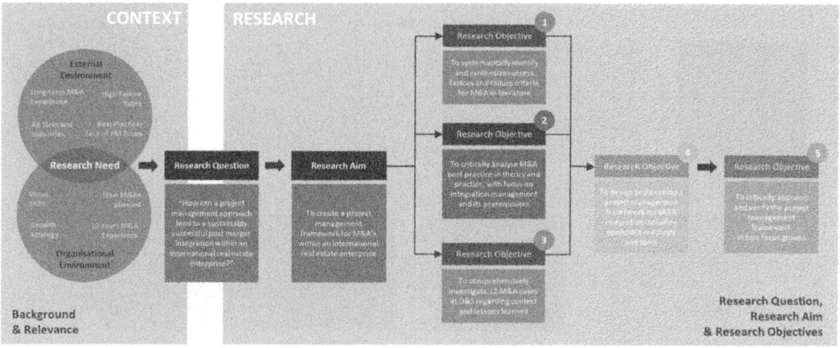

Fig. 1.3 Context and Research Approach

1.4 Research Focus

To support the nature of a strategic business consultancy project, this research has a strong and consistent focus on the applicability of all created results. This is evident throughout all following chapters, as both secondary and primary data led to tools and documents that aggregate, synthesise and transfer the collected knowledge and experience, to enhance organisational and personal capabilities in the field of M&A.

A precise definition of the scope provides transparency regarding focus and limitations of the planned research (Easterby-Smith et al., 2018). It is limited to international, friendly, horizontal mergers (Brekke et al., 2017) within a professional service organisation in the real estate sector (Fig. 1.4). Transferability to similar organisations is pursued, nevertheless, further research is needed on the transfer to bigger scale, different industries or hostile takeovers.

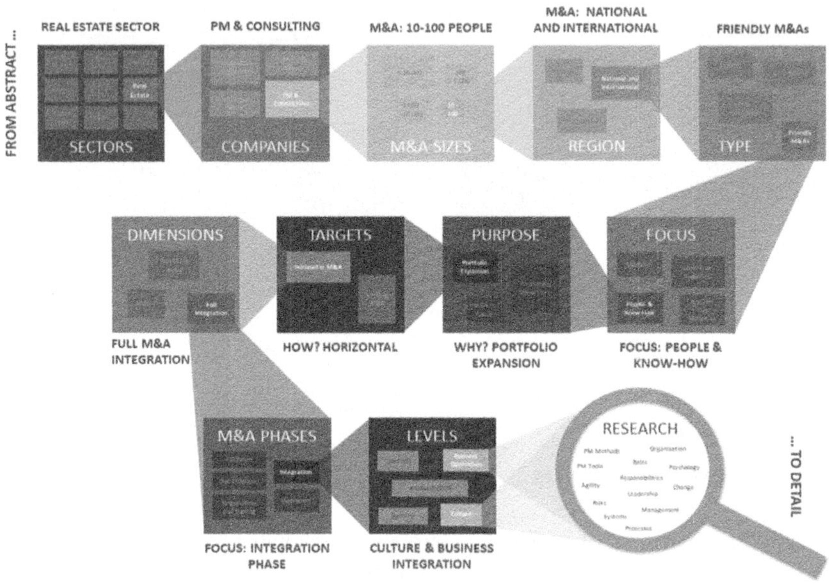

Fig. 1.4 Research Focus—from Abstract to Detail

2 Literature Review

The research objectives 1 and 2 require a deep engagement with the expert literature. This chapter examines peer-reviewed articles and books regarding concepts and definitions, reasons for success and failure and best practice for M&A integration and project management. The findings are continuously reflected against the context of D&S, to assure value and relevance for the framework development, and are synthesised in usable, transparent summaries as outcome of this integrative literature review (Torraco, 2016).

2.1 M&A—Background and Concepts

The phenomenon of M&A as the process of combining two previously separate firms (Haspeslagh and Jemison, 1991, cited in Lakshman, 2011) has been offering new strategic options for growth and diversification of organisations since the late 19th century (Nguyen, 2013). Since then, a development in several waves can be perceived (Meynerts-Stiller, 2019), leading due to globalisation especially since the 1980s to an increase in number and value (Fig. 2.1) throughout all industries.

The real estate sector plays a minor role in the M&A market, contributing to 4,5% in number and 5,6% in value to the total amount of deals since 1985 (Fig. 2.2). This is also evident in the literature sources, which are mainly based on other industries. However, the broad literature is relevant for all industries as the core findings are transferable and only little differences between industries and sizes are identified (Smeets et al., 2016; Steigenberger, 2017).

M. Miller, *Sprintegration®—An Agile Framework for M&A Integration*, BestMasters, https://doi.org/10.1007/978-3-658-37455-6_2

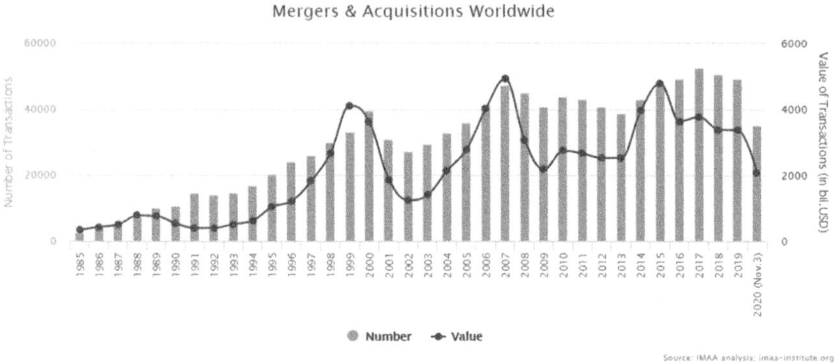

Fig. 2.1 Overview Global M&A Transactions (IMAA, 2020)

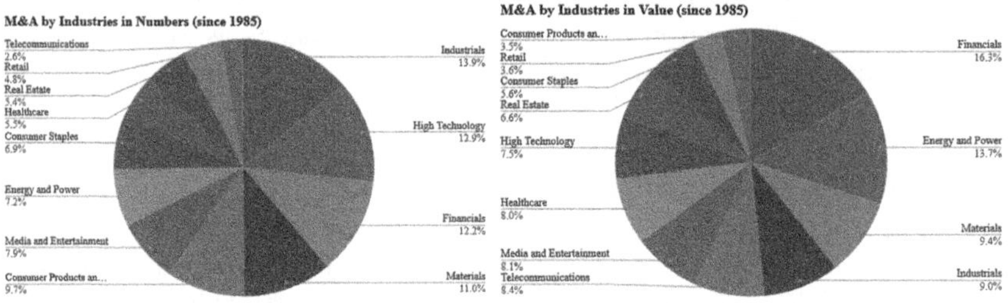

Fig. 2.2 M&A Transactions Breakdown by Industries (IMAA, 2020)

2.1.1 Definitions and Deal Structures

To understand the strategic decisions behind M&A investments, different concepts need to be distinguished. Although being often used interchangeably, significant differences between mergers and acquisitions need to be appreciated (Koi-Akrofi, 2016). Mergers describe the union of two organisations forming together a new company, whilst acquisitions represent transactions in which one company acquires another, for example through exchange of stocks, to gain control of the so-called target (Koi-Akrofi, 2016; Nazarian, 2017). Sherman (2018) confirms this definition by seeing mergers as two companies joining together as peers to form one new entity and acquisitions as one company buying another.

Different deal structures are applied depending on the deal's purpose, like share deals, where the shares of an organisation are partially or completely acquired including all rights and obligations, and asset deals, in which only specific assets are acquired, or carve-out deals, which represent transactions of one specific unit within an organisation (Sharma, 2016; Engelhardt, 2017). During the last ten years with increasing numbers of start-up companies, also tuck-in deals have evolved, in which smaller companies are acquired and integrated to gain access to new talent or products (Cotei and Farhat, 2018; PWC, 2020).

The context of D&S requires understanding regarding share deals, as this has been the approach in the past (see chapter 4). Additionally, the strategic focus on innovation mentioned in the introduction increases the relevance of participation in start-ups and tuck-in deals.

2.1.2 Reasons for M&A

M&As are undertaken for different strategic or opportunistic reasons by meanwhile 80 per cent strategic investors, also described as corporate investors, who strategically extend their operative business (Grimpe and Hussinger, 2007) compared to 20 per cent financial investors (Buschmann, 2019) like private equity investors with predominantly financial interest regarding return (Grimpe and Hussinger, 2007). This development must be seen in the context of the organisations' external environment (Brekke et al., 2017). Driven by increasingly changing, dynamic markets, framed with the term VUCA as acronym for volatile, uncertain, complex and ambiguous (Fu et al., 2018), companies need to react faster to changing conditions to stay competitive and maintain profitability and growth (Hromei, 2013). This exposes managers to decisions between organic growth through recruiting or extension (Fig. 2.3) or inorganic growth through, for example, M&A (Jansen, 2016; Achtenhagen et al., 2017). Required speed often leads to acquisitions (Högholm, 2016). Although it is not covering all strategic components or stakeholders, the following chart is suitable to demonstrate the decision path towards M&A.

The literature presents transactional deals or scale deals as one part of M&As (Buschmann, 2019; Rebner and Yeganeh, 2019), undertaken to increase efficiency, to exploit cost synergies or to create economies of scale (Tetenbaum, 1999; Hromei, 2013; Moeller and Brady, 2014), as functions become redundant or overhead can be reduced (Duvall-Dickson et al., 2016). Furthermore, scale deals can lead to increased market share and power enhancement (Moeller and Brady, 2014) and can weaken the competition (Hromei, 2013). However,

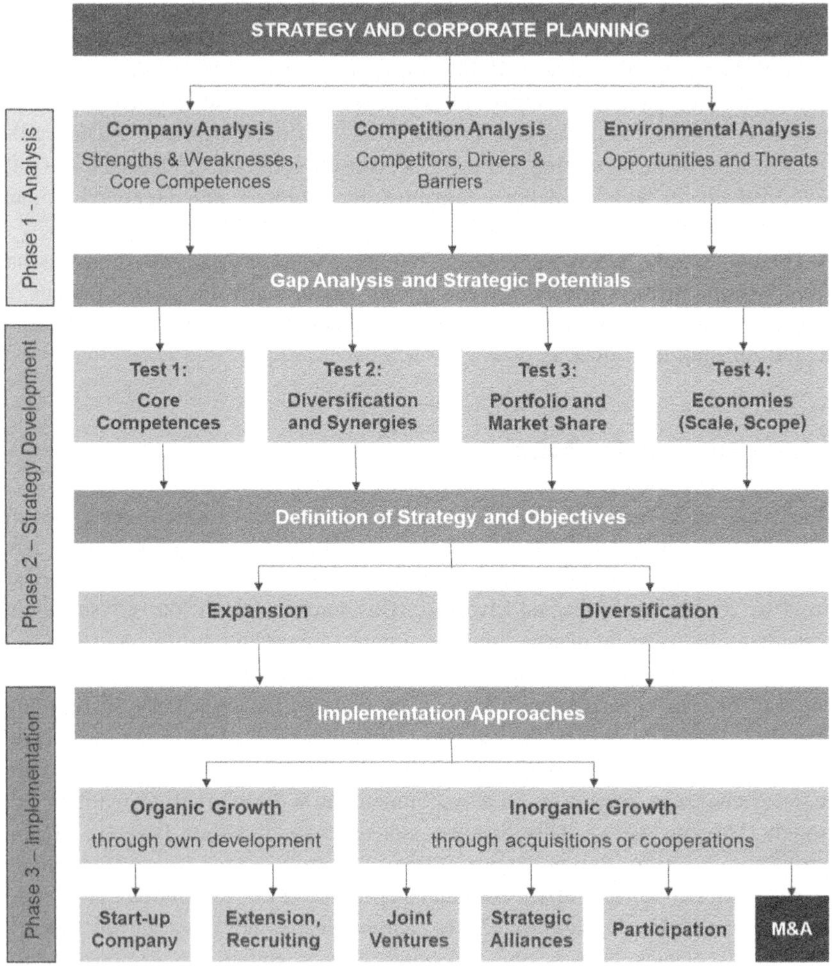

Fig. 2.3 Corporate Strategy Development. (adapted from Jansen, 2016, p. 212)

Meynerts-Stiller (2019) addresses a gap in literature by stating that synergies are often not clearly defined and therefore mostly linked to cost synergies, although they can also represent growth synergies.

Growth or revenue synergies focus on the market rather than on internal costs and lead to the second bigger part of deals with increasing importance during the last decades (Baird et al., 2019, cited in Buschmann, 2019), so-called scope deals.

Their focus is on gaining new resources and know-how, access to new distribution channels, products or market segments (Hromei, 2013; Brekke et al., 2017), and can lead through diversification to increased competitiveness (Duvall-Dickson et al., 2016). Compared to scale deals, which normally focus on organisations with the same or similar products or services (Rebner and Yeganeh, 2019), scope deals strive for adding new components. Similarly, innovation deals or transformational deals (Baird et al., 2019) can lead to a refreshed image (Hromei, 2013; Buschmann, 2019), internal restructuring or overall strategic transformation of the business (Moeller and Brady, 2014). Buschmann (2019) argues that scope deals are more complex than scale deals as they are less predictable, which is supported by other scholars (Baird et al., 2019; Rebner and Yeganeh, 2019). A recent study by PwC (2020) amongst managers of US companies presents that especially the people factor is a key challenge in scope deals, as meanwhile 65% see access to management and technical talent as a key driver, but only 17% perceive these goals as achieved.

Additional reasons for M&As are international expansion and access to new markets based on globalisation (Hromei, 2013; Meckl and Röhrle, 2016) or tax advantages (Hromei, 2013; Moeller and Brady, 2014). Furthermore and strongly related to risks for failure, M&As are sometimes conducted based on managerial self-interest, ego and power increase (Bhimani et al., 2015) and hubris (Zarb and Noth, 2012).

For D&S, acquisitions are undertaken primarily as scope deals to add complementary service lines and to enter new international markets, sectors or customer segments (see chapter 4). Furthermore, horizontal acquisitions within the same or complementary fields are realised rather than vertical acquisitions in which customers or suppliers within the supply chain would be integrated (Nguyen, 2013; Brekke et al., 2017).

2.1.3 M&A Process and Phases

Finally, an understanding of the M&A process is required. There is no standard definition of its phases (Engelhardt, 2017), however, the literature in total leads to a consolidated view of three main phases (Meynerts-Stiller, 2019) consisting of the Pre-Merger Phase, in which strategy and transaction goals are defined and the market is screened for potential targets, followed by the Transaction or Merger Phase, in which contact to the targets, detailed due diligence, negotiation of contractual conditions and price, business model development, signing and closing as well as integration planning are conducted, and the Post-Merger Phase, which contains the actual integration of the two organisations (Fig. 2.4).

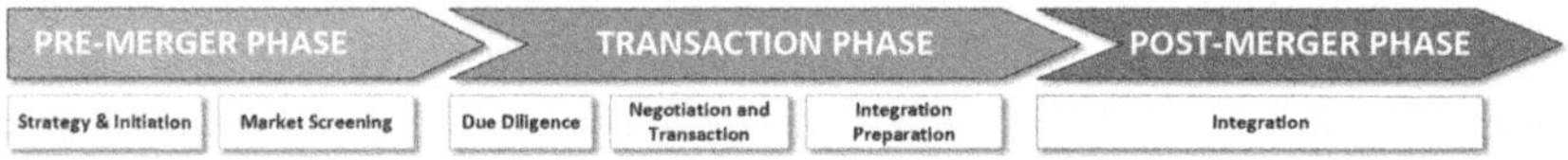

Fig. 2.4 M&A Phases. (adapted from Meynerts-Stiller, 2019, p. 48)

2.2 M&A—Reasons for Failure and Success

The previous chapter has equipped the reader with all basics to understand the following deeper analysis. Building on that, research objective 1 aims for the identification of reasons for failure and success in the literature. Therefore, this chapter elaborates the background of high failure rates and synthesises failure roots causes and success factors in an aggregated overview, which provides transparency about allocation and priorities and constitutes the basis for the framework development.

2.2.1 Failure Rates and Root Causes

Although they differ regarding focus or measuring methods, many researchers have analysed M&A failure rates with different results like 50 to 80 per cent (Nguyen, 2013; Koi-Akrofi, 2016; Spoor and Chu, 2018), supported by consultancy reports (PWC, 2016; EY, 2019), or even 70 to 90 per cent in the Harvard Business Review (Christensen et al., 2011). However, these statistics are criticised for inconsistency in data collection and success criteria (Nguyen, 2013; Meckl and Röhrle, 2016) and the high number of studies on M&A failure, summarising all scenarios of unfulfilled objectives or expectations, has the risk to lead to generalised assumptions of high failure rates (Anderson et al., 2012), evident in some articles that generally mention high failure risk without specific sources (Rozen-Bakher, 2018; Shi and Wang, 2020). Moeller and Brady (2014) even identify this issue as groupthink effect, in which positive statistics are ignored to confirm negative debates.

Nevertheless, all researchers state high failure rates (Fig. 2.5), Meckl (2016), for example, based on a meta-analysis of over 55.000 transactions.

The experts agree on a high risk of failure for M&As based on their complexity (Bhimani et al., 2015; Zhou et al., 2016; Steigenberger, 2017). Research on root causes is exhaustive and leads to cultural or human factors (Anderson et al., 2012), poor strategic rationales and communication (Koi-Akrofi, 2016), unrealistic expectations and too high buying prices (Christensen et al., 2011),

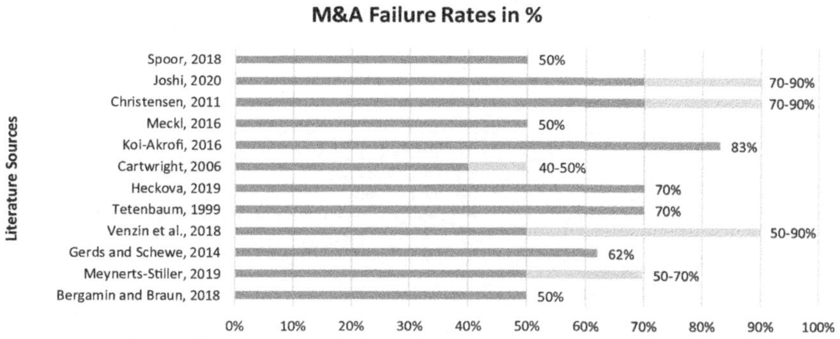

Fig. 2.5 Overview of Literature Sources on M&A Failure Rates

speed, competition, ineffective assessment models, self-interest in management (Fiorentino and Garzella, 2015) or lack of learning from previous cases (Zhou et al., 2016). The impact of culture on failure of M&A is controversially discussed and questioned by experts like Jansen (2016) arguing that the cultural differences are less relevant than the organisational conditions, supported by Bouwman (2013).

However, most researchers perceive the biggest risk for failure in an inadequately managed integration phase (Perry and Herd, 2004; Friedman et al., 2016; Steigenberger, 2017; Patel, 2018; Joshi et al., 2020). Furthermore, Friedman (2016) adds the prerequisites for integration success in previous phases, as further risks for failure are found in all stages (see Fig. 2.6).

In conclusion, based on the evaluation of 69 literature sources, the following reasons for failure are mostly mentioned:

- Incomplete due diligence, missing: culture and operations
- Management overconfidence, overoptimistic calculations
- Bad integration planning
- Lack of management experience
- Poor strategy rollout after closing
- Bad post-merger integration
- Weak synergy management
- Underestimated social issues, cultural clash
- Resistance based on emotions (fears, distrust), sabotage
- Human factors in integration

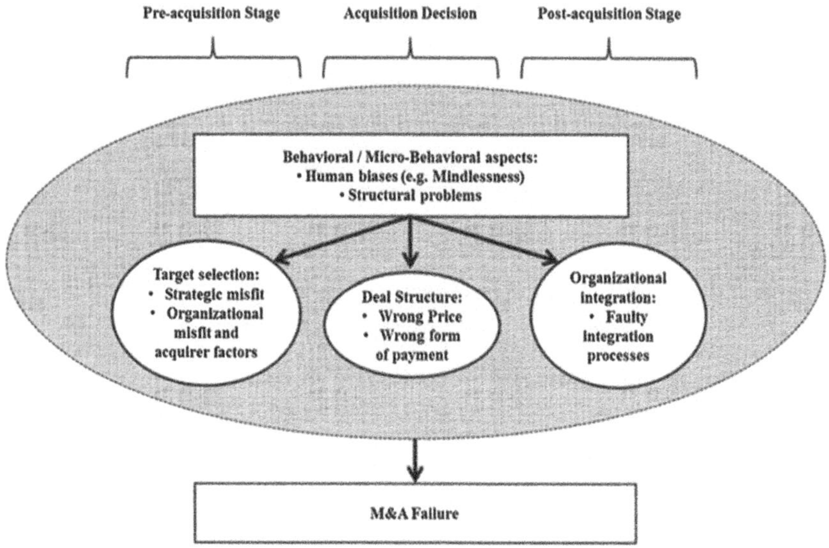

Fig. 2.6 M&A Failure Reasons (Friedman, 2016, p. 2342)

These reasons are highly relevant for D&S as a construction consultancy with strong people focus (Connaughton et al., 2015) involved in cross-border M&As with differences in language, power and working culture (Ahammad et al., 2016; Zhou et al., 2016).

2.2.2 Success Factors

In contrast to these reasons for failure, scholars identify success factors like identity creation (Joshi et al., 2020), clear business strategy (Christensen et al., 2011) or open communication and stakeholder involvement (Nguyen, 2013; Koi-Akrofi, 2016). Nevertheless, there is little guidance on how to achieve them. Even detailed concepts like mindfulness in leadership (Rebner and Yeganeh, 2019), knowledge-based cultural integration (Lakshman, 2011) or project management implementation (Hurta et al., 2017; Steigenberger, 2017; Patel, 2018) do not provide guidance on how these theories can be applied. This gap is also evident within D&S, as there is little transparency regarding the learnings from the previous M&As, so theoretical knowledge is not sufficiently accessible.

Overall, the literature presents a trend towards more focus on the human side of mergers (Zhang et al., 2015; Duvall-Dickson et al., 2016). Gerds and Schewe (2014) criticise phenomena like the merger syndrome for generalising the assumption of resistant, rejecting employees, and perceive organisational barriers as worse than willingness barriers, which is supported by Jansen (2016) and can be overcome through training, education and proper preparation (Venzin et al., 2018; Meynerts-Stiller, 2019)

The previously mentioned evaluation of 69 literature sources presents the following success factors as mostly mentioned:

- Clear strategy, vision, deal thesis, rationale, objectives
- External advisors for neutrality/objectivity
- Cultural due diligence
- No rigid plan, open to changes, iterative development
- Consideration of environmental changes, VUCA, complexity
- Mindfulness in management, high EQ, trust
- Continuous communication of goals, outlook, plans, impact
- Leadership with sufficient capacity, ethics, role-modelling
- Performance evaluation system, KPIs, reporting
- Dedicated, experienced integration manager
- Integration team from both organisations, promoters
- Knowledge management, exchange
- Focus on cultural integration
- Retaining key employees
- Identity and identification
- Organisational learning

2.2.3 Failure and Success Map

There is a vast literature on research objective 1. As this research strives for a high degree of applicability to bridge the gap between theory and practice, a failure and success map (Fig. 2.7) was developed. It provides transparency and overview regarding 69 evaluated articles and books and helps to prioritise them visually. The map allocates failure risks and success factors to process phases and involved roles or levels and grades them based on their frequency. Furthermore,

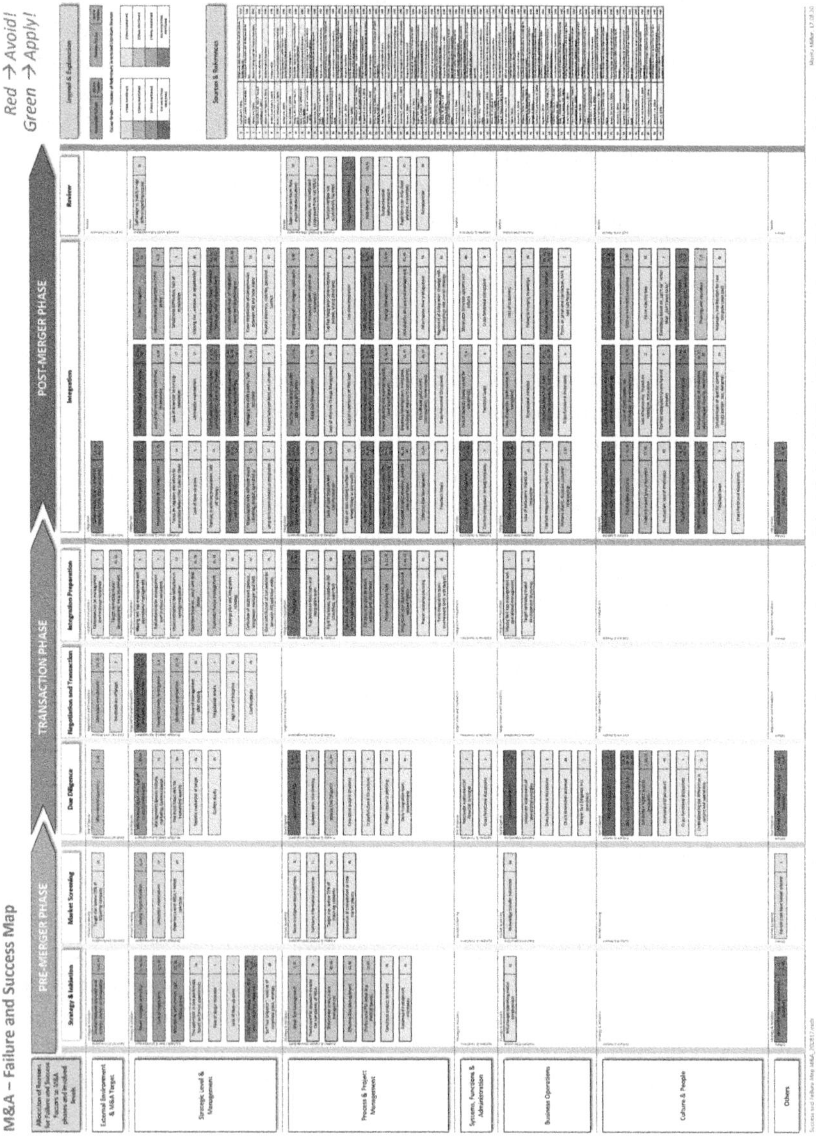

Fig. 2.7 M&A Failure and Success Map

this map can be used independently from the thesis document and contains all sources including embedded links. This reinforces the approach of an integrative literature review which aims for the synthesis of existing literature to create new knowledge (Torraco, 2016). This developed tool supports additional awareness and delivers scientific evidence as basis for discussions and decisions.

This evaluation visually underpins the focus on the integration phase and emphasises the importance of proper preparation, consistent strategy, project management and human factors. These elements will be further elaborated in the following sections.

2.3 Post-Merger Integration—Best Practice

As this sensitive phase is crucial for the success of M&A with the highest amount of risks (Steigenberger, 2017; Bergamin and Braun, 2018), research objective 2 elaborates best practice for the post-merger integration (PMI). Therefore, literature sources were examined regarding solutions or models for integration areas, degree and speed, roles and approaches for operational and cultural integration. These elements were selected due to their importance (see section 2.2.3) and relevance for D&S.

2.3.1 Areas and Levels of Integration

Bergamin and Braun (2018) emphasise the holistic consideration of all areas for the integration strategy (Fig. 2.8).

Although the previous M&As within D&S were undertaken as full integrations, especially regarding international growth the consideration of different degrees of integration might become relevant (Ahammad and Glaister, 2011; Jansen, 2016). A model for this decision, that many scholars like Larsson and Finkelstein (1999), Friedman et al. (2016), Steigenberger (2017) or Bodner and Capron (2018) have referred to, is the integration matrix developed by Haspeslagh and Jemison (1991). The classification of the degree of need for strategic interdependence and autonomy (Fig. 2.9) leads to a suitable integration approach with focus on value creation (Bodner and Capron, 2018).

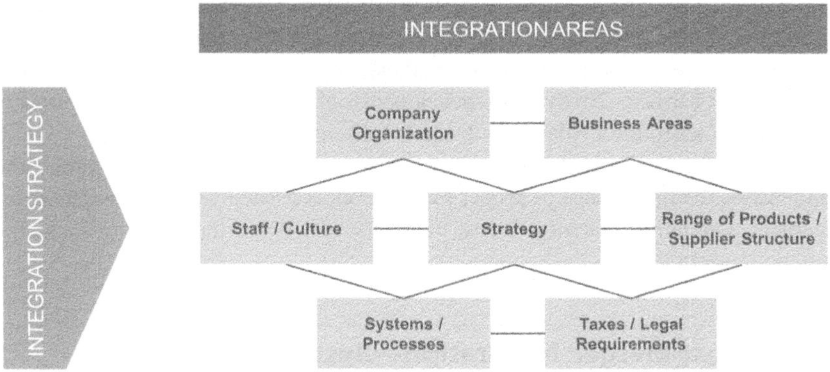

Fig. 2.8 Integration Areas. (adapted from Bergamin and Braun, 2018, p. 45)

Haspeslagh and Jemison (1991) distinguish between four approaches:

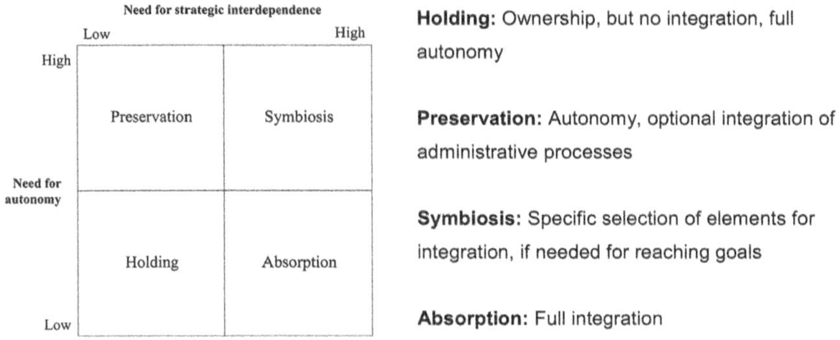

Fig. 2.9 Integration Matrix (Bodner and Chapron, 2018, p. 3, based on Haspeslagh and Demison, 1991)

This evaluation becomes even more relevant in combination with a second integration model. Whilst Haspeslagh and Demison (1991) focus on the business value creation, the culture end-state framework by Marks and Mirvis (1992, cited in Denison and Ko, 2016) identifies different levels of cultural integration, depending on the required change in both organisations (Fig. 2.10). This model also sheds a different light on the term of integration, often understood as a take-over (Meynerts-Stiller, 2019), whereas cultural integration actually requires change from both sides compared to assimilation (Denison and Ko, 2016).

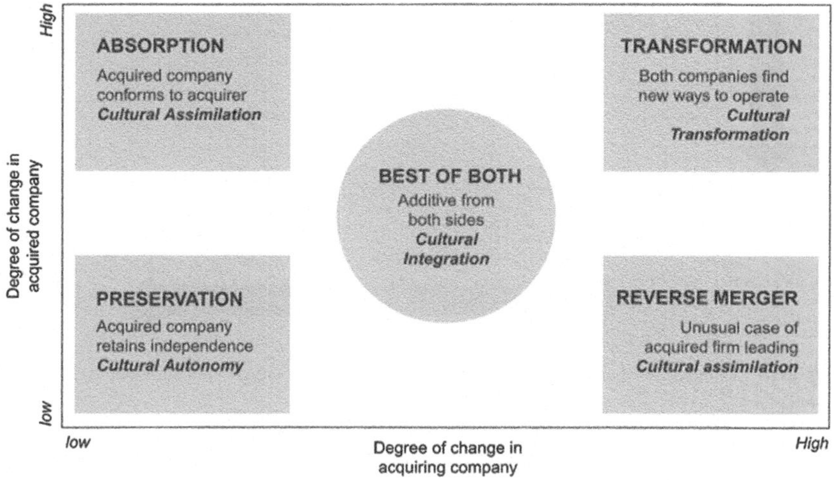

Fig. 2.10 Culture End-State Framework (Denison and Ko, 2016, p. 64, based on Marks and Mirvis, 1992)

These models can support awareness and decision-making regarding the appropriate level of integration for upcoming M&As within D&S, with different consequences in effort and risk (Buschmann, 2019).

2.3.2 Speed of Integration

The speed of integration is controversially discussed in literature. Whilst too slow integration can lead to a loss of momentum and to failure (Stone et al., 2000; PWC, 2020), too fast integration can result in overwhelmed employees and wrong decisions (Gerds and Schewe, 2014). Meynerts-Stiller (2019) argues that experience is required to know when fast and slow measures are appropriate. Gerds and Schewe (2014) emphasize on a conscious speed decision, as depending on the scope of change the level of speed increases complexity, which leads to difficulties in corrections and synergy risks (Fig. 2.11).

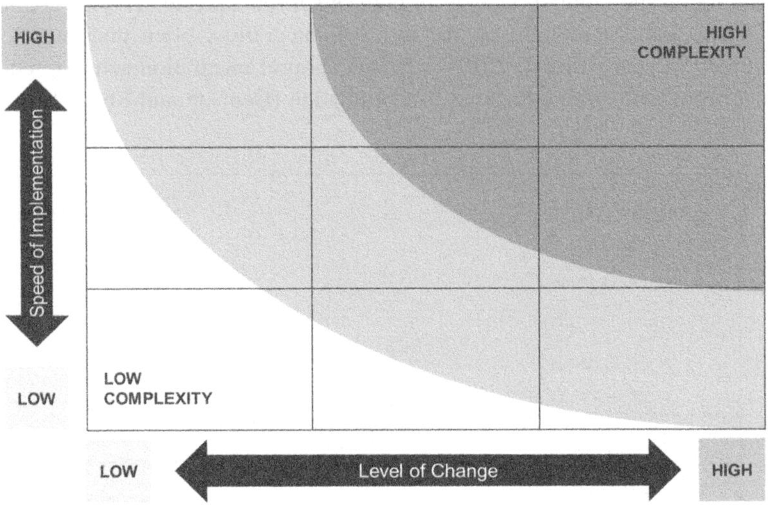

Fig. 2.11 Integration Speed and Complexity. (adapted from Gerds and Schewe, 2014, p. 47)

Venzin et al., (2018) use similar variables to differentiate between preservation, quick wins, gradual melting and radical integration (Fig. 2.12).

Combining both figures leads to a complexity classification of the integration strategies (Fig. 2.13), which support conscious decision-making, as already quick wins with low level of integration present at least a medium level of complexity based on their speed.

Gerds and Schewe (2014), whose book is based on a management survey examining integration success and evaluating what distinguishes successful managers from the average, conclude that speed itself is no success factor. However, top-performer dose the speed differently from the average by taking crucial decisions and changes like management positions very early (Fig. 2.14), afterwards decreasing the speed, but considering a longer integration duration than the standard 100 days of functional integration (Gerds and Schewe, 2014), which is supported by Bergamin and Braun (2018) stating that sustainable integration success takes much longer than 100 days. These findings can underpin early key decisions as part of the framework development.

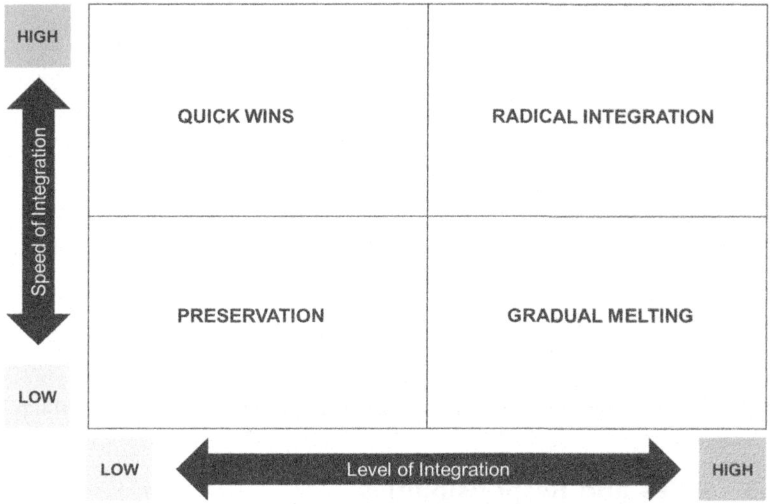

Fig. 2.12 Integration Strategies. (adapted from Venzin et al., 2018, p. 196)

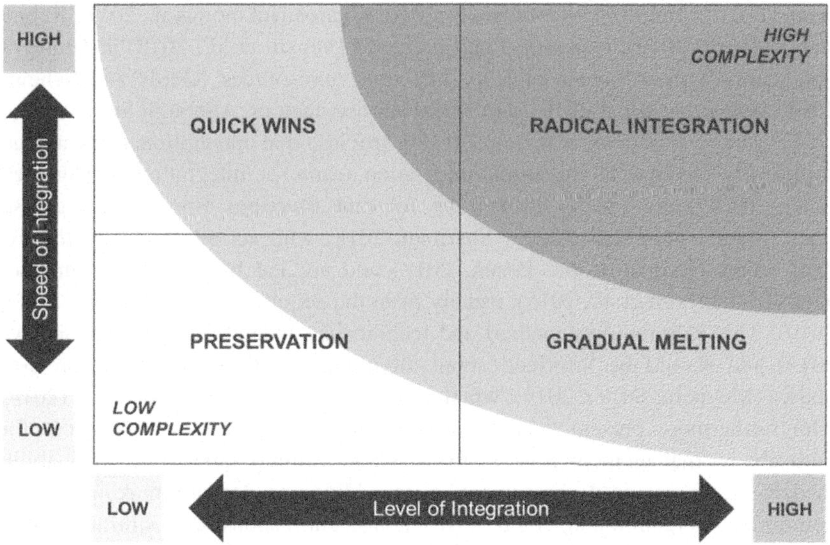

Fig. 2.13 Integration Strategies and Complexity

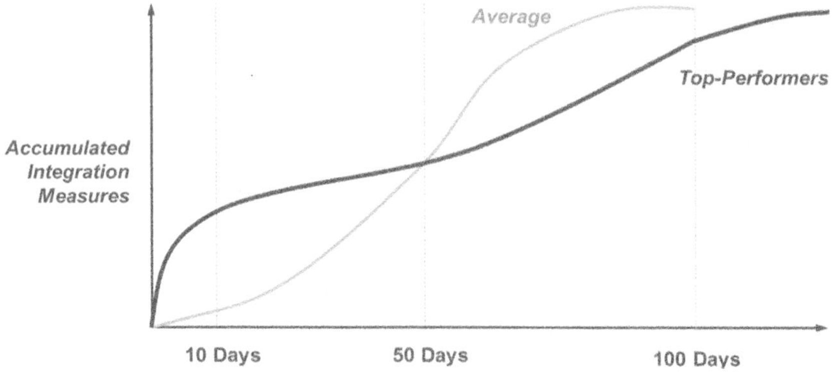

Fig. 2.14 Speed of Integration Measures. (adapted from Gerds and Schewe., 2014, p. 166)

2.3.3 Roles and Responsibilities

Furthermore, dedicated managers with strong leadership and communication skills (Waldman and Javidan, 2009; Maire and Collerette, 2011; Duvall-Dickson et al., 2016), mindfulness (Yeganeh, 2016; Charoensukmongkol, 2017; Rebner and Yeganeh, 2019), experience and presence (Venzin et al., 2018) and integration teams with sufficient capacity like time anresources (Gerds and Schewe, 2014; Meynerts-Stiller, 2019) are critical success factors. Although Steigenberger (2017) states, based on a review of 480 articles, that integration roles are not sufficiently covered in literature, integration teams or integration management offices (IMO) are ideally formed by relevant functions from both organisations (Stankiewicz-Mróz, 2015; Sherman, 2018) who act as promoters towards their teams (Bergamin and Braun, 2018) and are led by an integration manager (Trichterborn et al., 2015), usually from the acquiring side (Meynerts-Stiller, 2019). This role requires method and technical knowledge (Gerds and Schewe, 2014) and should be informed about all important decisions of the previous phases (Meynerts-Stiller, 2019), which is supported by Moeller and Brady (2014), who furthermore present deep knowledge of the acquiring company, comfort with chaos, management trust, emotional and cultural intelligence and ability to delegate as required characteristics. In addition, a decision-making steering committee (Bergamin and Braun, 2018), consistent responsibilities throughout all phases (Meynerts-Stiller, 2019) and early involvement of the operational management (Colombo et al., 2010; Lakshman, 2011) are positively related to success probability, and the different age of the sources shows their continuous relevance.

2.3.4 Knowledge Transfer and Cultural Integration

The field of approaches for operational and cultural integration is wide, however, one repetitively presented aspect has specific relevance for D&S. Knowledge management (KM) and exchange are critical success factors (Azan and Huber Sutter, 2010; Lakshman, 2011), also addressed by Spoor and Chu (2018), who suggest the creation of Communities of Practice (CoP) for knowledge transfer on collegial level. Gerds and Schewe (2014) state that what distinguishes top performers from the average is their consistent focus on training and education, supported by Schönreiter (2018). This implies that a joint purpose of the M&A (Stone et al., 2000) and close collaboration (Duvall-Dickson et al., 2016) support a natural merging of teams in their daily business.

Although employee fluctuation is a focus risk in the integration phase (Degbey et al., 2020), several experts argue that the pursued synergies can be achieved by only focussing on retaining key employees (Moeller and Brady, 2014; Zhang et al., 2015; Smeets et al., 2016). They form the anchor and contribute strongly to the creation of new identity and identification (Smith et al., 2013; Kroon and Noorderhaven, 2018; Joshi et al., 2020).

Bergamin and Braun (2018) furthermore highlight that knowledge transfer needs to go in both directions to exploit the full potential of the acquired resources.

This leads to the conclusion that in addition to planned workshops or events a key focus should be on knowledge exchange in the daily operational business, which supports both the achieving of the deal purpose and natural connection between the organisations.

If culture can be managed or integrated is also controversially discussed. Bischoff (2007) sees three conflicting assumptions as one reason for differing opinions on cultural integration.

- Objectivist Perspective: a company HAS a culture, which can be influenced
- Subjectivist Perspective: a company IS a culture, which evolves naturally
- Integrative Perspective: a company HAS and IS a culture and can partially be influenced

Following the integrative approach, cultural integration can be supported by agreeing on changing processes, structures and behaviours as cultural basis with low effort for adaptation (Meynerts-Stiller, 2019), based on the psychological levels in the pyramid going back to Dilts, Bateson and Whitehead (Fig. 2.15), related to Schein's cultural model (Schein, 2004).

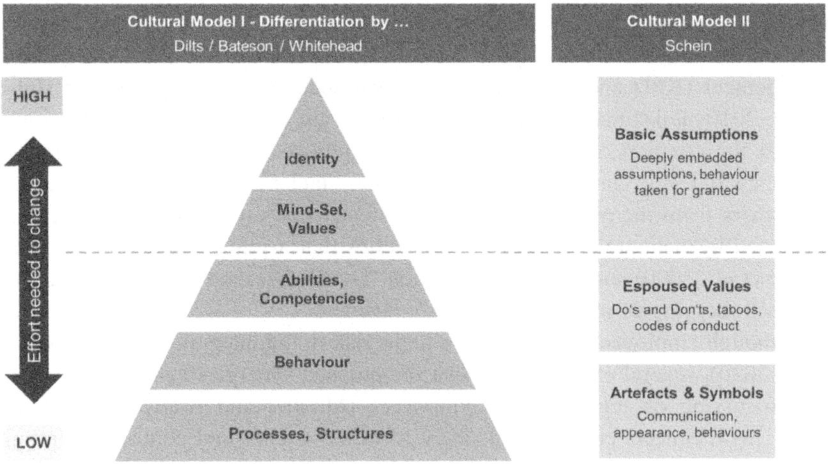

Fig. 2.15 Cultural Models. (adapted from Meynerts-Stiller, 2019, p. 199)

This implies that approaching these aspects first can create the common ground for joint values and new identity (Smith et al., 2013; Moeller and Brady, 2014).

Due to this high importance of psychological factors, many researchers recommend a guiding change management, preferably external, in addition to the business-oriented integration (Moeller and Brady, 2014; Rebner and Yeganeh, 2019) to lead through change curves (Fig. 2.16) that also occur in M&As (Meynerts-Stiller, 2019, based on Kübler-Ross, 1969).

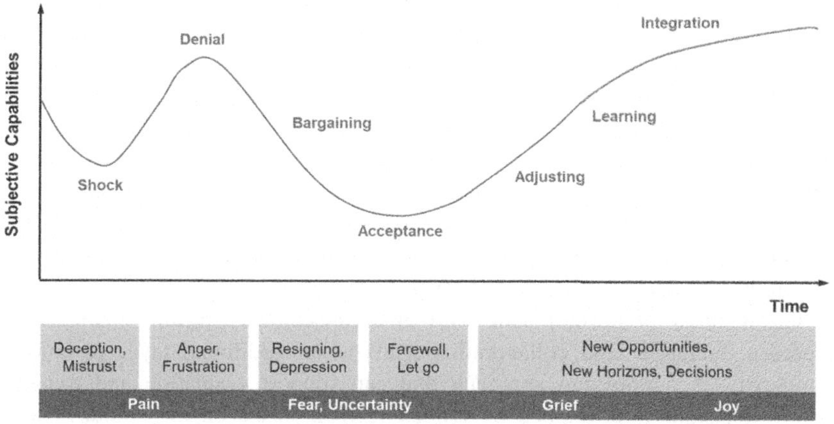

Fig. 2.16 Change Curve. (adapted from Meynerts-Stiller. 2019, p. 181, based on Kübler Ross, 1969)

2.3.5 Company Locations and Sizes

Knowledge exchange and daily collaboration are more difficult in cross-border acquisitions (Ahammad et al., 2016; Sharma, 2016). Nevertheless, the effect of culture and distance on M&A success is controversially discussed between scholars. Gerds and Schewe (2014) argue that the context is less relevant than expected and that CBAs do not have a lower probability of success, which is supported by Jansen (2016), but contrasted by Larsson and Finkelstein (1999) and Erel et al. (2012), stating that distance increases resistance and barriers in synergy creation, whilst similarity enhances the success probability (Stahl et al., 2011; Lee Marks et al., 2014; Joshi et al., 2020). Boateng (2019) reconciles the two positions based on a study of 209 international M&As, according to which cultural distance has a negative effect, however just in the short term view. In the long term, differences are accepted or dissolved (Durand, 2016; Boateng et al., 2019). The scholars agree that distance, language barriers, local cultures including behaviours, values and business practices require a higher degree of understanding during the DD phase (Perry and Herd, 2004; Hromei, 2013; Rebner and Yeganeh, 2019) and special attention during the integration (Tarba and Weber, 2011). This can be supported by company size, experience, differentiation in integration degrees and strong knowledge transfer (Ahammad et al., 2016), which closes the circle to the previously mentioned criteria.

Regarding company size, Nguyen (2013) states that a target size below 25 per cent of the acquiring company is critical for success, relativised to around 50 per cent by Nazarian (2017) based on the analysis of 3789 international transactions. It can be concluded that a bigger size of acquiring companies is common and increases the probability of success, which is in line with the approach of D&S having acquired smaller companies so far. However, an assessment of the organisational set-up regarding central functions is essential as smaller companies tend to have team structures with little overhead (Filipović, 2012; Högholm, 2016), and also the size and maturity of the local offices responsible for the integration need to be considered (Zhou et al., 2016; Huang et al., 2017).

The maturity or development level of organisations regarding management approach, hierarchy and collaboration leads to an additional layer of cultural complexity. A simplifying approach that can support evaluation and transformation decisions is developed by Laloux (2016). Based on the colour scheme of Ken Wilber (2000), Laloux (2016) defined stages of organisational evolution (Fig. 2.17), which could help to categorise and analyse the culture of buyer and seller and develop a joint vision.

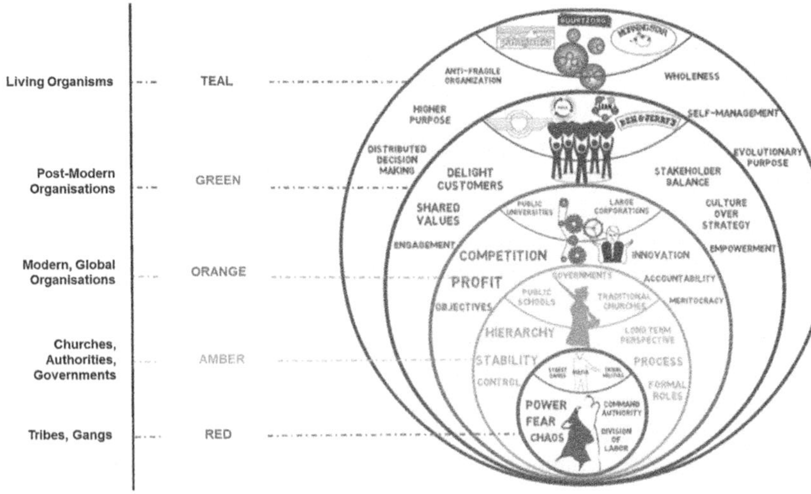

Fig. 2.17 Cultural Evolution—Development Stages (Laloux, 2016, p. 37)

2.3.6 Summary and Relevance

For future M&As at D&S, these prioritised aspects have to be considered and create a high level of complexity (Engelhardt, 2017; Bergamin and Braun, 2018). Especially due to the nature of an international, knowledge-based consultancy company with full dependency on employees, cultural layers of regional culture, organisational culture and maturity as well as personal values and behaviours are essential aspects to respect, and merging teams can be naturally enhanced through close collaboration and knowledge exchange, based on a joint focus on deal purpose and business value to create pursued synergies. The following chapter sheds light on different management approaches for this challenge.

2.4 PM for M&A

Being temporary endeavours undertaken to create unique outcomes (Project Management Institute, 2017), M&As need to be seen and dealt with as projects (Bergamin and Braun, 2018; Meynerts-Stiller, 2019) and require project management defined as application of knowledge, skills, tools and techniques to project activities to meet the project requirements (Project Management Institute, 2017). High failure rates related to integration management (Ficery et al., 2007; Koi-Akrofi, 2016; Joshi et al., 2020) justify an examination of the applied methods. This chapter will investigate theoretical models for the selection of PM approaches, leading to a reflection of traditional and agile methods.

2.4.1 Selection of PM Approach

Projects differ in addition to goals, timeframe, stakeholder, budget or location especially regarding their complexity (Cristóbal, 2017). Therefore several models support the evaluation of the degree of complexity in order to identify the best PM approach for the specific case (Abdou et al., 2016). Often used since its creation is the Stacey Matrix (Stacey, 1996), mainly in the version edited by Brenda Zimmermann from 2001 (Fig. 2.18, Cheek, 2016).

The classification of requirements agreement and certainty of methods leads to the evaluation whether a project is simple, complicated, complex or chaotic (Stacey, 2007). This model is often used together with the Snowden's Cynefin Model from 2007 (Snowden and Boone, 2007; Schirl-Boeck and Nachgabauer, 2019) to identify proper approaches for these categories (Fig. 2.19).

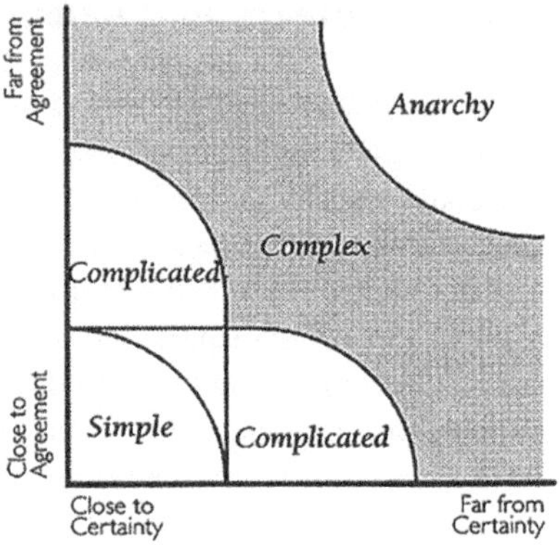

Fig. 2.18 Stacey Matrix (Zimmermann, 2001, p. 6)

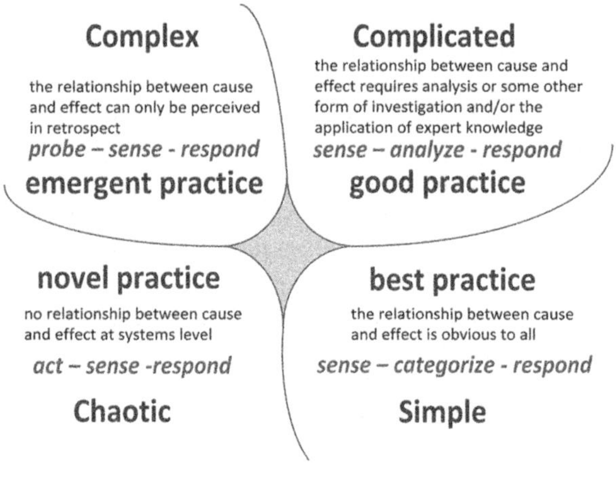

Fig. 2.19 Cynefin Model (Snowden and Boone, 2007, p. 4)

Transferred to M&A projects, complexity factors like dynamic environment, duration, number of stakeholders, speed or ambiguity of requirements (Poveda-Bautista et al., 2018), probability of changes and low predictability (Sohi et al., 2016) lead to a high degree of complexity. Scholarly contributions examining specifically the PMI complexity are rare and not recent, but still highly relevant. Lauser (2010) argues that especially the high level of changes for the people contribute to very complex processes, which creates a link to the previously elaborated levels of integration (section 2.3.1). Although they differ in complexity due to different degrees of change (Denison and Ko, 2016), predictability of outcomes is difficult in all scenarios (Steigenberger, 2017; Holbeche, 2019). Even though they do not explicitly differentiate between levels of integration, Engelhardt (2017) and Bergamin and Braun (2018) describe M&As as highly complex and dynamic, supported by Meynerts-Stiller (2019) stating that they are organisational, not linear projects, in which it is unpredictable what happens when two social systems are brought together.

A verification through the Stacey Matrix (Fig. 2.18) confirms these assumptions, as already a medium level of exact clarity of requirements and methods or approaches would lead to a complex project (Cheek, 2016).

This is given as often the due diligence doesn't cover all relevant components (Rebner and Yeganeh, 2019), so a complete picture evolves during integration, and environmental changes (Holbeche, 2019), long duration for synergy exploitation (Stone et al., 2000) and human factors (Dorling, 2017) make it highly unpredictable. Building on that, the application of the Cynefin Model would suggest that for complex projects consequently emergent practices need to be applied (Puik and Ceglarek, 2015), leading to rather agile and adaptive project management approaches (Mikkelsen, 2016), underpinned by Alami (2015) arguing that agile methods can support the reduction of project complexity.

However, one of the key findings of this literature review is driven by Patel (2019). Although the high complexity of M&As is confirmed, the applied methods and most literature sources still address it with traditional project management, rather suitable for simple or complicated scenarios (Mikkelsen, 2016; Patel, 2019). Patel (2019) developed an agile M&A approach (further elaborated in section 2.4.3), which is rare in literature, as the relation between complexity and agility in M&A is not sufficiently covered.

This means that one reason for failure including bad PMI management (Koi-Akrofi, 2016; Joshi et al., 2020) could be the fundamentally wrong management approach (Patel, 2019). The following sections examine the literature on traditional and agile M&A project management to validate this statement.

2.4.2 Traditional PM

The critique of Patel (2019) can be partially confirmed as many literature sources suggest traditional PM approaches for linear, predictable and controllable projects (Maire and Collerette, 2011; Sohi et al., 2016) like excel sheets, checklists and control tools (Bergamin and Braun, 2018; Meynerts-Stiller, 2019) or playbooks with a high percentage of standardisation of processes and routines (Venzin et al.,

2018; Meynerts-Stiller, 2019). This is also evident within D&S, as the process is mainly driven by traditional excel sheets with waterfall schedules. But, in contrast to Patel's statement, all scholars mention that they should not be applied rigidly (Venzin et al., 2018), that there is the risk of over-standardization (Meynerts-Stiller, 2019) and that iterative developments are required (Gerds and Schewe, 2014).

Other sources mention the need for PM for M&A (Meckl and Röhrle, 2016; Hurta et al., 2017), but without suggestions regarding methods. A rare detailed elaboration was undertaken by Reena Patel (2012) who argues that M&A project management should be based on the processes of the Project Management Body of Knowledge (PMBOK) by the Project Management Institute (PMI).

Despite the previously mentioned risk of rigidity, especially the holistic view of the knowledge areas (Fig. 2.20) supports a consistent PM approach (Meckl and Röhrle, 2016) and can contribute to the M&A framework development.

Fig. 2.20 10 Knowledge Areas PMBOK. (adapted from PMI, 2017, p. 25)

2.4.3 Agile PM

Nevertheless, Patel (2019) can be confirmed in identifying a lack of suggested methods for high complexity. Although scholars agree on the need for iterations (Gerds and Schewe, 2014; Jansen, 2016), agile processes (Buschmann, 2019) or openness for change (Bergamin and Braun, 2018), there is little guidance on how to achieve that and even less link to agile methods.

Patel (2019) argues that traditional approaches fail, as M&As are too complex and unpredictable, and developed an agile approach based on the agile manifesto (Beck et al., 2001) created by 17 software developers in 2001. They agreed on the need to approach changing requirements and software development processes differently (Sanchez et al., 2017; Hohl et al., 2018) and defined four core values (Beck et al., 2001):

- Individuals and interactions over processes and tools
- Working software over comprehensive documentation
- Customer collaboration over contract negotiation
- Responding to change over following a plan

Patel (2019) translated these agile principles to M&A by combining them with Scrum as the most commonly applied agile framework (Rasnacis and Berzisa, 2016), also based on software development (Cervone, 2011; Preußig, 2018). The core idea is that products are developed iteratively in time-boxed sprints, which create an increment of the final product that is reflected, tested, and further developed (Schwaber and Sutherland, 2017). Furthermore, Scrum includes clear roles and responsibilities within self-organised teams and provides them with tools, artefacts and events like sprint planning to select prioritised tasks for the upcoming iteration, sprint review to collect feedback on the product, and sprint retrospective to reflect on process and collaboration within the team, with focus on continuous improvement (Schwaber and Sutherland, 2017).

Based on interviews with M&A experts, Patel (2019) developed a set of so-called plays, which are events and project management tools, embedded in an overall game plan for synergy creation and successful integration (Fig. 2.21), based on collaboration, early planning, transparency and ability to deal with changes (ibid.), which still requires translation and adaptation within the specific organisational context.

Holbeche (2019) observes that companies are generally struggling with becoming agile, supported by Brueller et al. (2014), who furthermore state that M&As could even facilitate strategic and organisational agility if managed properly.

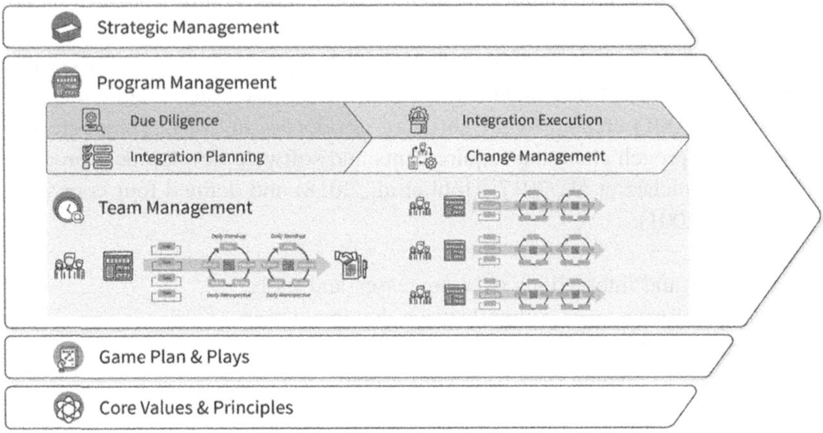

Fig. 2.21 Full-Scale Agile M&A Integration Model (Patel, 2019, p. 73)

Bringing these findings together leads to support for Patel's approach, although the implementation might be difficult as it means a change for management methods applied over decades (Holbeche, 2019). A transfer to M&As can enhance collaboration and knowledge transfer in both directions (Junni et al., 2015), which was previously identified as key success factor (Gerds and Schewe, 2014; Spoor and Chu, 2018).

Preußig (2018) emphasises that agility needs to be understood as mindset and values rather than a fixed system, supported by Hohl (2018). Nevertheless, the creation of detailed roles, events and tools based on methods like Scrum facilitates a successful implementation (Denning, 2019), which underlines the focus on applicability of this research.

2.5 Summary and Conclusion

Although literature is limited regarding the specific context of the real estate sector and small M&A sizes within consultancies, the broader analysis provided very important insights for D&S. To cover both international and regional research, global scholars and experts from Germany were included, however, the addressed topics and methods do not provide substantial differences. The evaluation of M&A concepts and reasons for failure and success (RO1) has led to a specific focus on the integration phase regarding culture, knowledge management, roles and environmental influence factors and to the evaluation of complexity and M&A project management (RO2). It can be concluded that for the context of D&S especially human factors and knowledge transfer approaches are essential, based on strong project management (Fig. 3.1). As agile approaches address the high complexity better than traditional methods, this will be taken into consideration for the framework development. Although the literature is vast regarding M&A, it is shallow regarding guidance and practicable tools for the integration phase, especially regarding agility. This underpins the need for an applicable holistic project management approach for M&A, which is the driving purpose of this research.

3 Methodology and Methods

Reflection on personal assumptions regarding nature of reality and knowledge creation can positively impact research quality and creativity (Easterby-Smith et al., 2018; Taguchi, 2018). The general preference would lead to interpretivism through exploration of individual subjective situations, behaviours and experiences (Saunders et al., 2019), supported by the results of the reflexive tool HARP (Bristow and Saunders, 2014). However, the specific research context and aim to develop an applicable framework led consequently to a different methodology, which the HARP tool suggested as second preference.

3.1 Research Philosophy

The paradigm of this research, as the philosophical assumptions that define a researcher's actions and worldview (Lincoln et al, 2011, cited in Kaushik and Walsh, 2019), is pragmatism. While reconciling the objectivist and subjectivist ontologies by making it dependent on context and research question whether observable phenomena or subjective meanings or both constitute the relevant knowledge (Saunders et al., 2019) and which methods are applied (Smaling, 1994), pragmatism focuses on solving practical problems in the real world (Kaushik and Walsh, 2019) by applied research and emphasis on research problem and context. Initiated by the philosophers Pierce, James and Dewey end of the 19th century (Sil, 2008), pragmatism rejects predetermined theories of ontology, epistemology and axiology, and argues that meaning can only be derived from lived experience (Easterby-Smith et al., 2018) and that value of science is anchored to its ability to resolve genuine human problems (Martela, 2015), to support sustainable actions (Ruwhiu and Cone, 2010). Methodology and methods for a specific research depend on the best way to address the research question,

M. Miller, *Sprintegration®—An Agile Framework for M&A Integration*, BestMasters, https://doi.org/10.1007/978-3-658-37455-6_3

which could lead to positivist or interpretivist positions (Smaling, 1994). However, for this specific research the epistemological standpoint goes rather towards interpretivism with subjectivist ontology (MacIntosh and O'Gorman, 2015) due to the subjective evaluation of the different unique M&A contexts and personal perspectives (Saunders et al., 2019). As elaborated before, the outcome that this research aims to achieve is the practical implementation of an M&A framework, based on the analysis of the specific context and individual, personal experiences within M&A cases. Furthermore, emphasis on value-driven research (Kim and Donaldson, 2018) and reflective involvement of the researcher, related to the planned insider research (Finefter-Rosenbluh, 2017), underpinned this approach.

3.2 Research Approach and Strategy

Although a pragmatism approach allows different research methodologies, the specific research context led to an inductive, qualitative and exploratory approach. As mentioned before, there is no sufficient theory available which could be tested or verified for the specific research problem, so this theory needed to be created and inducted to the world of knowledge (Saunders et al., 2019). The importance of organisational context and individuals involved in M&A clearly supported a qualitative research approach that explores and observes experiences, feelings, attitudes and values through in-depth interviews (Florczak, 2017; Easterby-Smith et al., 2018) and collects data to understand and interpret pitfalls and success factors, leading to a new, applicable framework. The overall research strategy was not only a single case study at D&S as an organisation, but a multiple case study through the analysis of 12 individual M&A cases, which supports a higher confidence in representativeness and transferability of the findings (Gustafsson, 2017). However, it was no pure case study approach, as the primary data collection also included external experts, without involvement in the internal M&A cases, to contrast and compare experiences.

3.3 Methods and Ethics

Based on the extensive, integrative literature review (Torraco, 2016), which established credibility and helped to predefine themes (Saunders et al., 2019), semi-structured in-depth interviews were conducted, with the main concern to review, complement, confirm and contract the meanings that the participants assigned to certain phenomena within previous M&A cases. Interviews can provide fresh, rich data and enable researchers to explore experiences that may not be available in literature (Rubin and Rubin, 2012). Semi-structured interviews were appropriate as they provided insights into decisions or opinions of the interviewees through open questions including the possibility to ask deepening questions and to react to situational observations like hesitation, facial expressions or clarifying inquiries from the participants (Cooper and Schindler, 2014).

The previous literature review provided insights into M&A risks, success factors and best practice approaches, which were mirrored against the experiences of 55 interviewees. The conducted interviews contributed to the elaboration of RO3 (examination of 12 M&A cases regarding context and lessons learned) and furthermore completed the RO2 by shedding light on best practice in real cases and expert perspectives (see also section 1.3).

These findings together with the concluded integrative literature review results were synthesised in an applicable PM framework including detailed roles, systems and methods.

The applicability of the framework was verified with M&A experts and consultants in focus groups, which served to examine reactions and collective discussions (Saunders et al., 2019) and were therefore helpful to collect feedback on the final results and their implementation. Two focus groups were formed to cover the quality review holistically. On the one hand, the process architecture regarding roles, workshop concepts, information flow, change and agility was reflected with a focus group consisting of both external and internal process consultants. On the other hand, content and internal collaboration were discussed with the current PMI team formed by representatives of all central functions, who were involved in all previous M&As within D&S. This reflection of process and content was crucial for the overall aim of applicability.

3.3.1 Sampling

The purposive sampling, as the process of selecting research participants based on the researcher's judgement (Florczak, 2017), represents the high level of heterogeneity within the previous M&A cases of D&S regarding size, country or services and aims furthermore for integration of external expertise. To create useful results for different environments and to consider the late data saturation due to the heterogeneity, this led to the decision to involve a high number of 55 interviewees (see Table 3.1), consisting of managers and employees from 12 M&A cases, representatives of all central functions and external M&A experts.

Table 3.1 Purposive Sampling

Purposive Sampling	Research Participants		Selection Criteria	Aim and Focus	Main Themes (a priori)	Specific Themes (a priori)	Organisation
Drees & Sommer	Operative Units	Management	Involved in D&S M&A, personal contact, existing relation, trust and openness	Management perspective on M&A process (acquiring + acquired side), personal experiences	• Personal role and background • Definition of working culture • Involvement and role in M&A cases • Goals and communication • Stakeholders • Requirements collection • Integration management • Success and impact evaluation • Improvement potentials • 5 main lessons learned for M&A • Additional comments and ideas	• Cultural integration • Business integration	**14 Participants** Interviews, 60-90 min. Semi-structured, virtual
		Employees		Employee perspective on M&A process (acquired side), personal experiences			**15 Participants** Interviews, 60-90 min. Semi-structured, virtual
	Central Functions	HR, F/C, TQM, Marketing, IT		Administration perspective on M&A process (acquiring side), personal experiences		• Standard approach or indidual solution? • Key questions in Due Diligence phase • Involvement and role in M&A	**12 Participants** Interviews, 60-90 min. Semi-structured, virtual
External Experts	M&A Consultants		Experts in M&A, personal network	Theory and consulting approaches, methods, best practice		• Standard approach or indidual solution?	**9 Participants** Interviews, 60-90 min. Semi-structured, virtual
	M&A Managers		Responsible for M&A in other companies, personal network	M&A approaches within different organisations, transferability check			**5 Participants** Interviews, 60-90 min. Semi-structured, virtual

The external view provided by both M&A consultants and M&A managers from different organisations supported the comparison between organisations and completed the holistic picture on best practice for integration management. Pilot interviews within all groups allowed reflection and adjustments in content and scope (Majid et al., 2017).

3.3.2 Preparation and Administration

All participants were contacted personally and received research brief, participant information sheet, interview questions and consent form to assure confidentiality, anonymity and consent in data usage. All interviews were conducted virtually as video conferences, which allowed despite distance observations of vocal and facial expressions (Salmons, 2015). Audio records, field notes and transcripts supported the analysis. The focus groups were conducted as virtual workshops, neutrally moderated to receive feedback on the applicability, without leading the groups into any direction (Gill et al., 2008).

3.3.3 Analysis

The rich qualitative data was structured, reduced and coded in order to support the interpretation and thematic analysis (Taguchi, 2018; Saunders et al., 2019). This was enabled by a detailed template analysis as appropriate approach to identify patterns and themes and to iteratively develop the findings with an evolving template (Brooks and King, 2014). Furthermore, template analysis allows preselected a priori themes (see Table 3.1), which were reflected in interview questions, and the content structure of the interviews supported the analysis, as it pre-ordered the themes (Dougherty et al., 2019) and helped to allocate and categorize the codes accordingly (Fig. 3.1).

Saldaña (2009) highlights the importance of the interrelations between categories and themes as outcome of proper coding, to identify the abstract theory on a higher level. Detailed coding and allocation to relevant themes were crucial for this research, to transform the high amount of data into useful conclusions and findings.

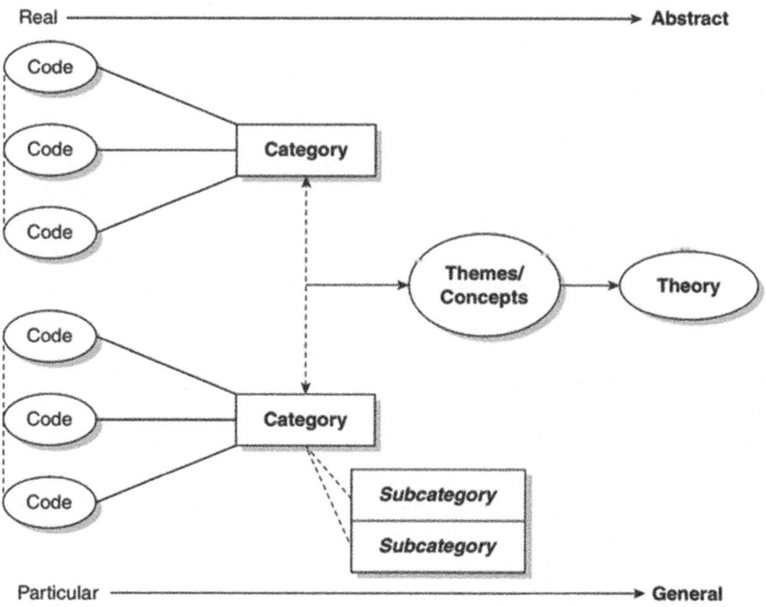

Fig. 3.1 Codes-to-Theory Model for Qualitative Inquiry (Saldaña, 2009, p. 12)

The amount of interviews also allowed quantification of qualitative data (Wojatzki et al., 2019) through autonomous counting (Hannah and Lautsch, 2011), for example how often certain themes or codes were addressed by which groups (Elliott, 2018). The high number of participants from different roles and groups enabled several cross-comparisons of perspectives, for example examined grouped results according to M&A case, management and employee role or national and international locations.

This approach was in line with the pragmatist epistemology (Kaushik and Walsh, 2019) and contributed to the research objectives 1, 2 and 3 (see section 1.3) by combining collected primary data with secondary data from reviewed literature. The analysis of the focus groups led even more pragmatically to the actual framework and its further improvement, supporting the pragmatism emphasis on high-quality practical solutions to overcome the risks of M&A failure for D&S.

The data will be safely stored for three years. Validity and reliability of the results were furthermore secured by iterative reflection of literature, external expertise for specific topics and by consultation of the participants regarding approval or redaction (Mero-Jaffe, 2011).

3.3.4 Ethics

Compliance with research ethics is a major duty of researchers (Kim and Donaldson, 2018; Saunders et al., 2019). All relevant aspects for this research were addressed with specific measures (compare Table 3.2). The interview documents covered all ethical requirements, which were verbally emphasised at the beginning of every interview. This supported transparency about expectations and created trust, to increase the probability of honesty (Britten, 2007). All documents and their compliance with ethical and legal standards went through approval processes by the involved supervisors.

The ethical considerations also covered the specific requirements of insider research. Although it supported access to knowledge and personal reflection of the insider (Finefter-Rosenbluh, 2017), challenges like role duality, conflicts of interest or pressure through legitimate power needed to be considered (Mercer, 2007).

This bias was minimised by selecting participants based on personal contact with strong trust level, who were fully informed about purpose and outcome of the research and who could not be harmed personally based on anonymity and confidentiality.

Table 3.2 Research Ethics Concept

Research Ethics	Measures for Implementation – Insider Research at Drees & Sommer
Voluntary participation	Defined in consent form and information sheet and communicated by researcher
Right to withdraw	Defined in consent form and information sheet and communicated by researcher
Confidentiality	Defined in consent form and information sheet and communicated by researcher
Anonymity	Data is analysed and stored in anonymous way without names, neutral content
Harm avoidance	Anonymity is secured, critical content will be neutralized, no consequences possible
Independence of researcher	Clear communication about impartial, objective researcher role in introduction
Privacy	Consent is required for audio-recording, transcripts are sent for approval or redaction
University research ethics	Ethics approval process through supervisor before start of research
Company guidelines	Compliance guidelines are followed (business ethics), external participants are asked
High quality	Content approval through supervision for interview questions and data analysis
Psychological safety	No judgements, open and respectful conversation in safe environment (safe zone)
Reduction of bias, scepticism	Clear communication about purpose, aims and benefits of the research
Pressure avoidance	No participants with direct leadership connection are selected, free and open choice
Trust, openness, honesty	Selection of participants with existing personal relation and trust basis for honesty
Personal interests (insider)	Reflection about identity and perception with supervisor, awareness about neutrality

To none of the participants there was or is a personal power or influence relation by the researcher, which supported the free choice of participation (Britten, 2007). As reflections on M&A integration touch sensitive topics like fears, failure or conflicts, the feeling of safety was essential to access the required depth of insights for high-quality results, which required high interviewing skills (Rowley, 2012; Majid et al., 2017).

4 Findings

The overall research goal of applicability led consequently to extensive primary data collection through interviews with practitioners. The internal M&A cases' heterogeneity regarding location, size, services and time resulted in the analysis of experiences in 12 M&A cases to generate substantial findings, which cover the different perspectives of both management and employees of the individual entities and the corporate units (Fig. 4.1). These findings were reflected against the expertise and best practice contributed by external M&A consultants and managers for comparison and inspiration. Fig. 4.1 furthermore makes transparent that the 5 German and 7 international cases had a predominant size between 10 and 40 employees and cover a constant development over 6 years including all learnings.

The following sections summarise the findings with the highest relevance for the framework development and combine the qualitative evaluation based on template analysis methods with basic quantification approaches which support the prioritisation, followed by the results of the focus group workshops with the objective to gain feedback on the framework's applicability. The participant coding system assures the anonymity and all participants' statements are referenced in these codes (for example II.4).

M. Miller, *Sprintegration®—An Agile Framework for M&A Integration*, BestMasters, https://doi.org/10.1007/978-3-658-37455-6_4

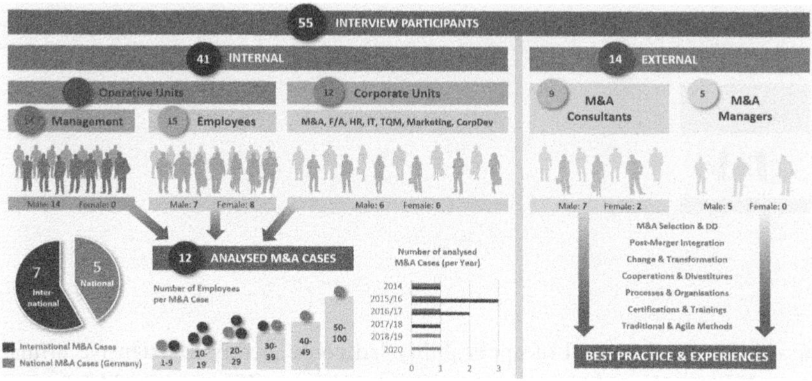

Fig. 4.1 Interview Participants and M&A Cases

4.1 Reasons and Objectives

Although the analysed 12 cases provided many differences in their context, they were predominantly undertaken as scope deals (10 of 12 cases) with the purpose of portfolio extension, new capabilities or to gain access to new markets (Fig. 4.2). The remaining cases were scale deals focussing on scaling effects within existing markets. This underpins the previously mentioned growth strategy of D&S, especially towards internationalisation.

All M&As were undertaken as friendly mergers, however, the analysis of the different perspectives of buyer and seller demonstrated different reasons behind these steps. Whilst for D&S portfolio extension, growth, capabilities and revenue synergies were deal drivers, the smaller sellers aimed for organisational cost synergies, succession planning, access to bigger projects or staff development opportunities. This is primarily related to the size of the acquired companies, as the size of 20 to 40 employees is a turning point towards more structures and processes (I.4, I.6, I.13). The M&A drivers overlap in the joint purpose of entering new markets and creating business synergies and cross-selling opportunities (I.12, I.14, I.17, II.1).

Significant findings during the discussions of M&A objectives were the participants' critical views on strategy and communication. The interview question towards communication of these M&A reasons showed many improvement potentials. 56% of the interviewed operative participants criticised a lack of overall vision and strategy, a lack of communication (28%) and even wrong communication regarding the expected change (14%), which underpins the high importance of strategy and communication identified in the literature review. This was supported by the external experts identifying lack of communication (43%) and a lack of strategy (29%) in their internal or consulted cases, which makes this a general issue, and by the internal central units missing transparency and understanding of the big picture (50%).

Fig. 4.2 Overview Findings—M&A Objectives

4.2 Culture

Previously identified as one crucial success factor, the consideration of organisational and local culture was an important interview focus, supported by participants classifying culture as the central topic for employees (I.14, I.26, II.6, III.8) or as underestimated and highly success relevant (I.1, I.7, II.2, III.6, III.13). The evaluation of statements on culture, cultural differences between buyer and seller and general cultural diversity provided transparency about the categories used to describe culture, the differences of public image and self-image of D&S and roots of cultural differences (Fig. 4.3). Mirrored against the cultural model by Dilts, Bateson and Whitehead used in the literature review (section 2.3.4), it can be identified that the participants described corporate culture primarily through addressing processes and structures (40%), followed by behaviour and atmosphere (20%) and mindset and values (19%), whilst abilities and competencies (9%) or identity (12%) were associated more rarely.

The internal participants' perspectives demonstrate substantial differences between the self-image of long-term D&S employees and the public image perceived by the M&A partners. This is especially evident in the perception of processes and structures, described as dynamic with flat, little hierarchy, and contrasted by the external perspective seeing them as rigid, less agile and more hierarchical compared to their own organisations. Furthermore, differences can be identified in the degree of autonomy and freedom and the self-image of strong values, from external perspective partially perceived as not lived. Accordance can be found in profit and quality focus, strong German roots and a high level of employee responsibility. The cultural diversity within D&S has increased over the last years due to different locations, services, sizes and M&A integrations. 14 participants addressed already during this question the need of cultural due diligences (CDD) as required improvement potential.

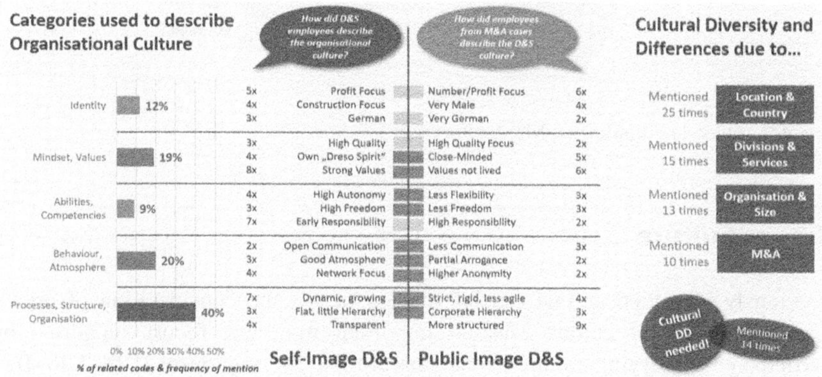

Fig. 4.3 Overview Findings—Organisational Culture

4.3 PMI Management

As this research focusses on a successful management of the integration phase, the evaluation of the responses regarding the integration phase had a high relevance for the framework development. Both general organisational topics and specific measures regarding functional, operational and cultural integration were discussed and requirements and suggestions were compiled. On the one hand appreciation for a smooth system integration (I.17, I.27), learning curves in the central units and business workshops or cultural events (I.9, I.12) became obvious, on the other hand the majority of statements was critical about the integration management (Fig. 4.4). This is mainly evident in high numbers of internal participants stating a lack of clear vision and goals, no active management, missing plan and orientation, and mostly lack of active measures towards operational and cultural integration. Furthermore, some participants stated language barrier (I.2, I.13) and a too dominant, imposing attitude as well as little understanding of differences as hindering aspects during the integration (I.9, I.22).

Without active question from the interviewer, the participants reflected on requirements and ideas for a successful PMI phase, which demonstrated a high level of personal engagement and interest in this topic. No significant differences between the learnings from the internal cases and the external experts' opinions could be identified, which underpins their relevance. In addition to the missing components mentioned before, practical measures like change management, holistic DD, joint projects and collaboration, transparent and adaptive plans and learning from previous cases were suggested, including a strong emphasis on the soft aspects and values like eye-level, understanding and respect, driven by a strong leadership of the management and clear roles and responsibilities, further elaborated in the following section.

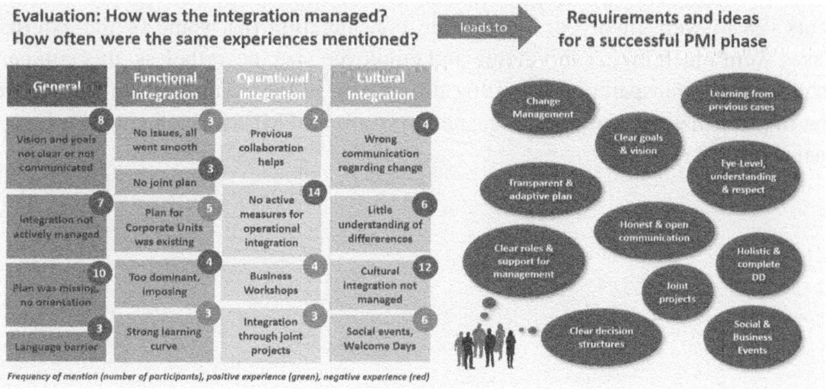

Fig. 4.4 Overview Findings—Integration Management

4.4 Roles and Responsibilities

The analysis of involved roles and organisational set-up for the M&A process provided transparency of major differences between the internal approach and the experts' approaches in other organisations (Fig. 4.5), which implied learning potentials. Internally, every M&A case was driven by deal partners, however mostly fading out after signing. The integration responsibility in all cases was with the local or division management, often described as left alone with this additional task (I.6, I.11, II.7). With growing experience, the central units formed a PMI team for functional M&A integration, however, without representation of business or cultural components or operative staff. Only in two cases the operational integration was led by integration managers. An operative PMI manager, locally present, well connected and experienced within the acquiring company (I.7, I.19), with strong method and communication skills (II.5, II.9) as well as capacity and management support (I.2, I.25) was described as key improvement need by 16 participants. Furthermore, a hesitating approach towards external support (M&A consultant in only one case, no external change management) is evident.

Despite being similar regarding management responsibility, this approach was contrasted by the external M&A consultants and managers, who mentioned functional PMI teams with PMO structure overseeing the individual functional workstreams as present in 93% of the described cases, and especially dedicated operative PMI managers in 85% of the cases. Also lower in number, but in several cases external M&A process consultants (36%) and change management consultants (28%) were involved. Taking into consideration that some of the external cases were much bigger in volume and employee size, nevertheless, this comparison leads to transparency regarding differences in the organisational set-up and the improvement potential of dedicated operational PMI management and change management.

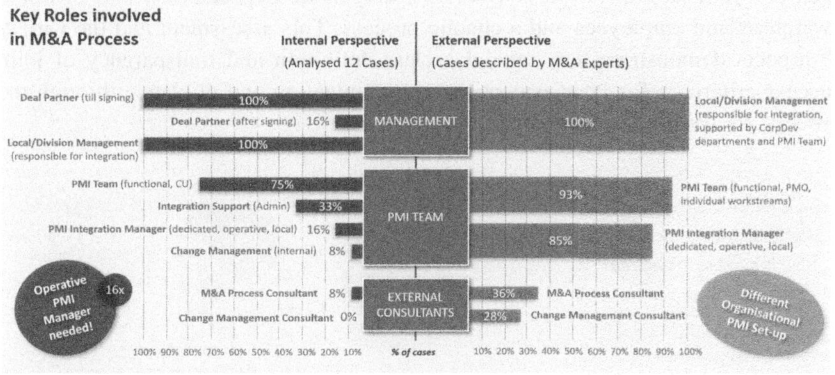

Fig. 4.5 Overview Findings—Roles and Responsibilities

4.5 Success Evaluation

As this research aims for sustainably successful integration management, the definition of success criteria and the evaluation of the success of previous cases are essential. Although the 12 cases differ regarding the degree of success, no major differences between the subjective perspectives of management, employees or the central units regarding the general success of the M&A cases could be identified. However, the criteria differed considerably (Fig. 4.6). Whilst the interviewed managers as well as the corporate units measured success predominantly against growth, profit, revenue synergies, brand impact or new project opportunities, the employees added career opportunities, daily business processes, identification, knowledge transfer, network and attitude as success criteria. Significant was furthermore that the success of M&A for all participants was not only measured against the final results, but also against the process, evident in critique towards the imposed standards, weak integration management, lack of transparency and leadership or weak communication.

Five cases were described as successful by all associated parties, six cases were evaluated as partially successful and one case was perceived as rather not successful. The strengths of the successful cases were seen primarily in growth, portfolio match, profitability, employee retention or access to new markets. These aspects were also mentioned in partially successful cases, however, reduced by weak processes, imposing attitude, second class feeling, lack of exchange, weak communication or too slow execution. The less successful case was assessed as such due to a lack of business synergies, unrealistic expectations, loss of brand awareness and employees and a chaotic process. This assessment and the variety of aspects demonstrate how crucial a clear definition and transparency of joint success criteria is for later evaluation, communication and guidance through the process, to avoid pure subjectivity.

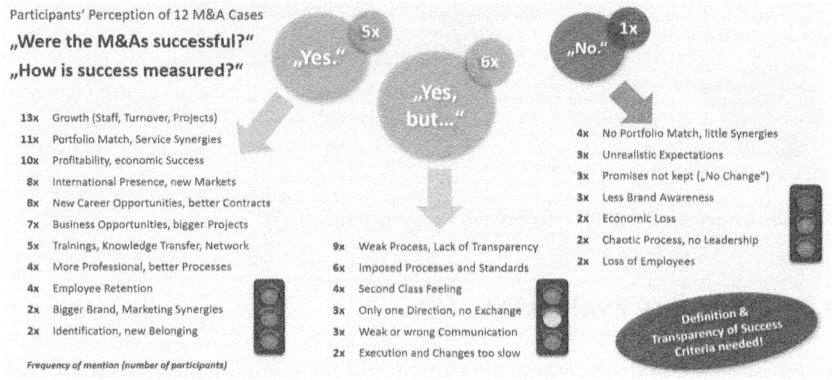

Fig. 4.6 Overview Findings—Success Evaluation

4.6 Lessons Learned and Best Practice

Finally, the participants were asked to reflect on best practice, improvement needs and general lessons learned as transferable results. Although the variety of subjective learnings and recommendations was very rich, the quantification provided transparency regarding the prioritised aspects (Fig. 4.7). The statements were compiled according to their belonging to general organisation, functional, operational or cultural integration and assessed regarding how many times certain themes were addressed. This section presents which measures were seen as prioritised success factors for M&A by both internal and external participants. No substantial differences between the statements of internal participants without M&A expertise and the external participants and their expert approaches could be identified. This suggests that the overall priorities have a certain degree of transferability and importance for all cases.

It can be summarised that a strong majority of the 55 participants perceived a joint and holistic integration plan (39/55), transparent strategy and goals (31/55) and open and honest communication (29/55) as the most important general aspects, followed by a dedicated integration management (23/55) and clear concepts for system integration (27/55), operational integration (22/55) and cultural integration (26/55).

Furthermore, the cross-evaluation of lessons learned and recommendations throughout all interview questions has shed light on the importance of the personal, soft aspects and the dependency on leadership, attitude, respect and openness. The importance of culture was evident in most participants' contributions and conclusions, which leads to the finding that the functions, operations as well as organisational and local culture need to be seen as a whole from a holistic view, rather than focussing only on functional or business integration neglecting the other aspects. This interdependency was a crucial finding for the framework development.

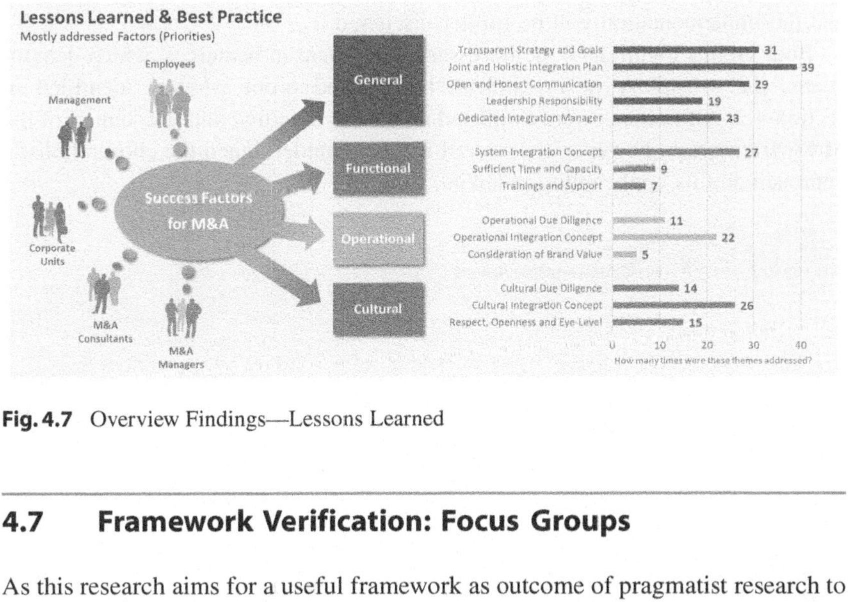

Fig. 4.7 Overview Findings—Lessons Learned

4.7 Framework Verification: Focus Groups

As this research aims for a useful framework as outcome of pragmatist research to overcome a practical problem, feedback on applicability and completeness plays a crucial role, anchored in RO 5. Therefore, two focus groups with different perspectives were involved and contributed to the development. Both sessions were arranged as virtual workshops, with presentations of research findings and framework components followed by questions, ideas and feedback, visually documented in a virtual workshop tool and allocated to the respective topics.

The first focus group was formed by internal and external operative process consultants with focus on process architecture, required change and overall framework logic. Key findings from this session were a perceived high level of completeness and detail of the developed systems and a confirmation of the required changes. Whilst the experts supported a project approach, a focus on decision patterns and a breakdown into subprojects, they suggested further steps like a cost and benefit analysis or exit scenarios, which are not part of this research (Fig. 4.8).

The second focus group represented all corporate units of D&S and focused on the practical applicability of the framework for the company-specific context. With high appreciation for the results, especially the identification of an operational integration manager, the required stronger collaboration with the operative units and the development of sub-processes for different scenarios were addressed and the implementation will be further discussed.

Both groups highlighted the necessary investment in resources, which demonstrates the sensitivity of investment, budget and profit, already identified in section 4.2. All findings were evaluated and led to detailing and fine-tuning of the M&A framework, however, the overall feedback underpinned the chosen holistic approach and its applicability potential.

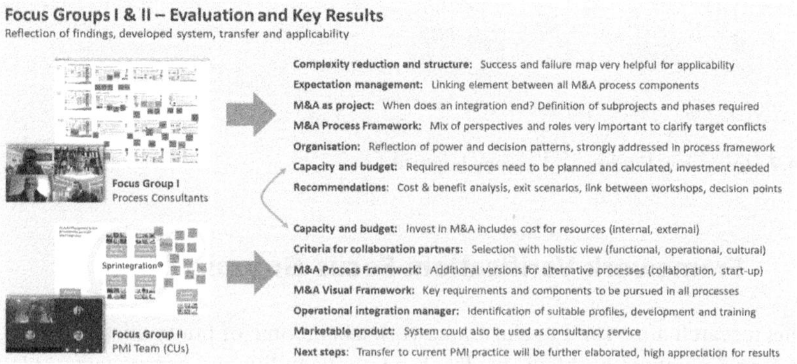

Fig. 4.8 Overview Findings—Focus Groups

4.8 Summary

The extensive primary data collection facilitated an overview of 12 M&A cases and individual focus topics predefined as a priori themes, completed by external experiences and approaches. In conclusion, transparency about strategy, goals and success criteria, communication, awareness and consideration regarding multi-dimensional culture, integration plans and clear measures, dedicated roles and a holistic DD could be identified as themes that were evident across most interviews. Synthesising all statements related to values and behaviour throughout all interview questions underpinned the importance of soft human factors like respect, eye-level, openness and personal behaviour for the sustainable integration success. Furthermore, the examination of the primary data shed light on the strong personal involvement and engagement of the participants in this topic, which could be observed in the time spent for the interviews, a high number of ideas and improvement suggestions and deep personal experiences, which enriched the findings essentially.

4.9 Best Practice Map

The overall aim of applicability of all results led also for the primary data to a synthesised and aggregated overview of all findings, which allows prioritisation and supports awareness and decision-making. Therefor a map of best practice and lessons learned for M&A integration was created (Fig. 4.9), covering the most frequently mentioned topics and their sources as well as individual suggestions and ideas. Both the most important items and the specific measures inspired the framework development described in the following chapter.

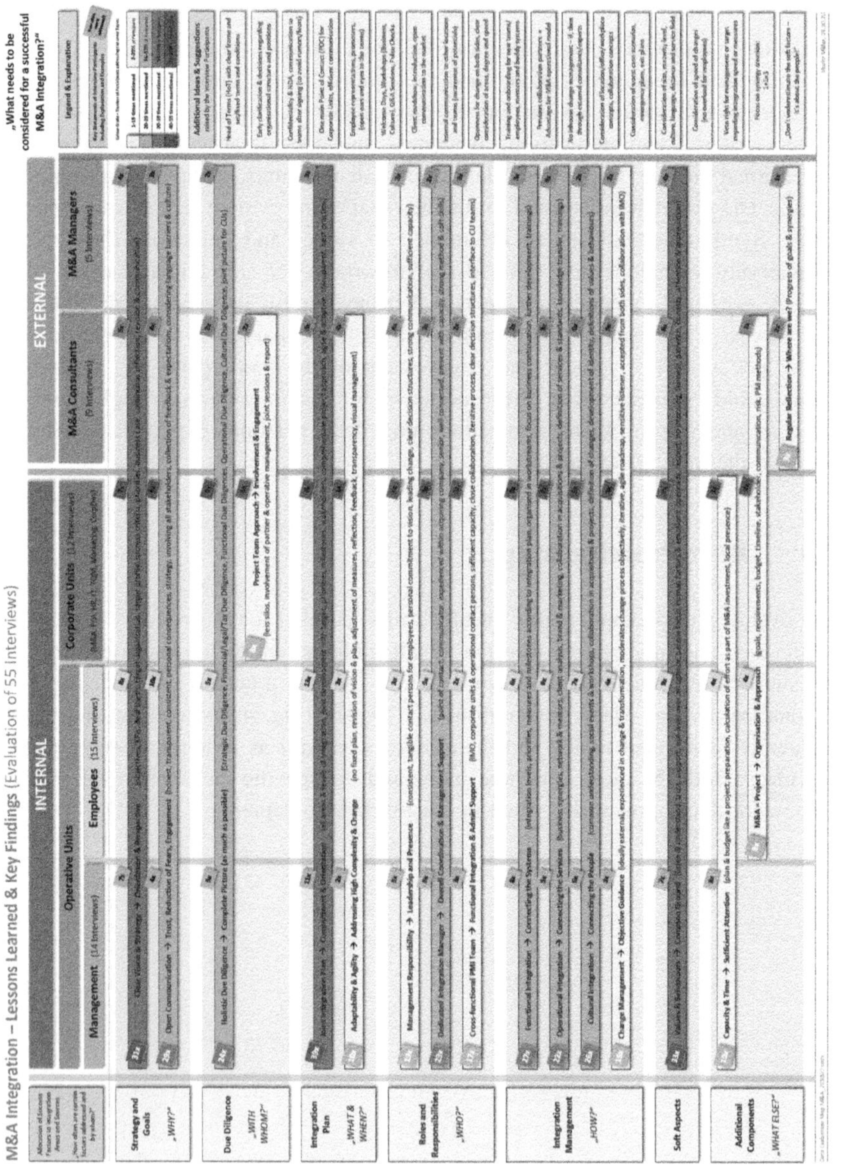

Fig. 4.9 M&A Integration—Best Practice Map

Discussion and Framework Development

5

The previous chapters have provided an overview of success factors, risks and management approaches for M&A integration from literature sources and the detailed examination of practical M&A cases and best practice contributed by M&A experts. This formed a rich database and covered comprehensively the research objectives 1, 2 and 3. The following sections will lead the reader through the process of synthesising and aggregating this data and the development of three framework levels:

- **Visual Framework:** Required components for successful M&A integration
- **Process Framework:** Transfer to company-specific M&A process
- **Sprintegration®:** An agile M&A integration management system (roles, methods, tools)

These developments constitute the core of the research results and fulfil the research objective 4 as well as the overall research aim to create an applicable framework for M&A integration. Therefore, the findings from secondary and primary data were compared and examined regarding similarities and differences and synthesised based on identified priorities.

Continuous quality checks for all development increments and iterations were undertaken by comparing them to the success and failure map from the literature (section 2.2.3) and the best practice map from the interviews (section 4.9) to assure that all critical factors are integrated and considered. The focus groups completed this development process through their detailed feedback. This reflective approach led to the pursued high level of applicability and relevance for the specific organisational context.

M. Miller, *Sprintegration®—An Agile Framework for M&A Integration*, BestMasters, https://doi.org/10.1007/978-3-658-37455-6_5

This chapter presents the developed frameworks chronologically as vehicles to discuss the findings from literature and interviews and their implications for the practice. Overall, a high accordance between these data sources can be observed, with only minor differences in the interpretation of culture, complexity, agility or the importance of size and distance of M&A targets, however, the key results from the literature review were strongly supported and confirmed by the collected primary data. This underpinned their relevance and strengthened the definition of framework components. Furthermore, the interviews allowed to investigate certain areas in detail which were only covered superficially in the literature, especially regarding the specific company context and the requirements of a knowledge-based international consultancy. All developments are linked, build upon each other and allow practitioners to deal with the complexity of M&A projects, considering the specific and limited context of this research (see section 1.4). All components can be extracted, which supports the achievement of high applicability without requiring a detailed reading of this document.

5.1 Visual Framework—Components for M&A Success

The identified key success factors observed in the evaluation of secondary and primary data were aggregated and illustrated in a visual framework, which was continuously iterated (Fig. 5.1). It does not only utilise the image of a building, it also follows the same logic. Certain layers and steps need to be created successively and build upon each other, whilst the columns need to stand in parallel, with the same quality and attention, to bear the load of the roof. However, the quality of the ground underneath is ultimately essential for the building's long-term stability. This logic was reflected and transferred to the M&A context and individual components will be explained in detail in the following sections.

According to literature, a clear purpose, strategy and defined, measurable objectives constitute the basis of successful M&As (Colombo et al., 2010; Meckl and Röhrle, 2016), which is explicitly supported by the interview participants, associated with orientation and perspective for all stakeholders through consistent communication and continuous adaptation to environmental changes (addressed in 31 interviews). Whilst early involvement of the target in the creation of a joint vision and operational models was highlighted by several scholars (Lakshman, 2011; Gerds and Schewe, 2014) and supported by interviewed M&A consultants (III.9, III.12), the involved operative managers were more focused on transparency of expectations and commitment of the strategic management (I.11, I.14, I.19).

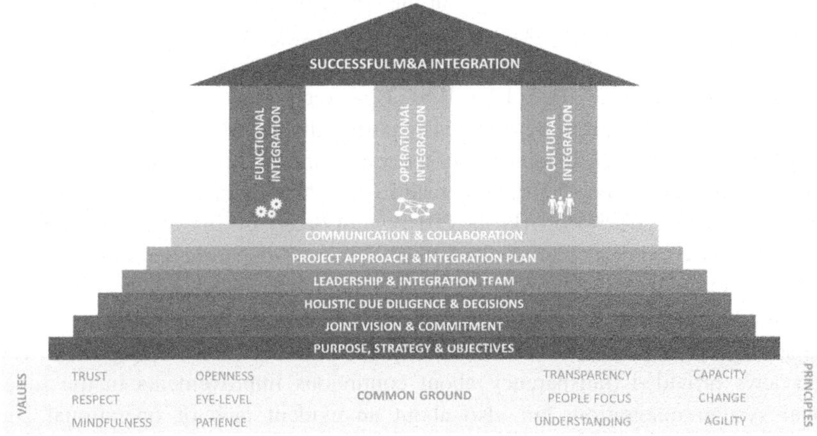

Fig. 5.1 Visual Framework—Components for M&A Success

Both the interviews and the literature furthermore highlighted the dependency of consistent integration decisions on a holistic due diligence, however, the interview participants only provided rough ideas on which topics should be covered and how. Here the literature served as source for operational and cultural due diligence concepts (Stone et al., 2000; Joshi et al., 2020), which enriched the process framework. In accordance with scholars like Hromei (2013) or Rebner and Yeganeh (2019), the interviews have shed light on the importance of leadership as key management responsibility in the M&A integration process and of a dedicated integration team. Especially a dedicated operative integration manager was identified as improvement potential through comparison of internal and external practice (compare section 4.4), underpinned by Moeller and Brady (2014) or Gerds and Schewe (2014). Furthermore, a project approach based on the knowledge areas of PMI (Patel, 2012; Hurta et al., 2017) supports a comprehensive set-up and minimizes the risk of underestimating aspects like scope definition, communication, resource planning or stakeholder management. This was supported by several interviews which demonstrated that the integration was often not handled with the same priority and awareness as external projects (I.15, I.23). Many participants missed a transparent integration plan, which should according to the literature be adaptive, flexible and not rigid (Meynerts-Stiller, 2019; Patel, 2019), and the interviews added the focus on its joint development with the target as a frequently mentioned component (addressed in 39 interviews).

Finally, a key success factor throughout the whole process is transparent communication with a continuous focus on goals and strategy (Sherman, 2018; Venzin et al., 2018), exchange of feedback (I.20, I.26, II.10) and consideration of cultural and language differences (I.2, I.10, II.8). Both regarding the due diligence and the integration preparation, but especially during the actual integration phase, all actions should foster collaboration as natural measure for knowledge exchange (Azan and Huber Sutter, 2010; Spoor and Chu, 2018) and resistance reduction (Zarb and Noth, 2012; Koi-Akrofi, 2016), reinforced by interview participants perceiving M&A projects as ideal platform for cross-departmental collaboration (II.2, II.11) and opportunity to break up functional silos (I.17, I.28).

A successful M&A integration phase (Fig. 5.1) depends on an equal awareness and strong measures towards functional, operational and cultural integration. The interviews provided transparency about continuous improvements in the functional system integration, but also about an evident lack of operational and cultural integration concepts (section 4.3). The operational integration can be driven by joint projects, knowledge exchange and joint service developments (Schönreiter, 2018), which is supported by several interview participants who added specific business and culture events as important milestones (I.12, I.25, II.1, II.3, II.5). Although the importance of culture and location is discussed controversially in the literature (see sections 2.3.4, 2.3.5) and several researchers have doubted the direct influence on integration success, the primary data evaluation would rather support scholars like Erel (2012) or Larsson and Finkelstein (1999) who observe culture, language and location distance as big barrier. This is supported especially by the examined international cases, where these differences caused misunderstandings and second-class feelings (I.8, I.10, II.5), which implies that for international M&As even higher attention is required. Overall, this holistic approach also contributes to organisational learning (Bhimani et al., 2015; Hečková et al., 2019) by allowing individual stakeholders to understand the bigger picture and other workstreams' responsibilities, which leads to joint solutions and can improve the everyday collaboration, also independently from the M&A processes (I.28, II.12).

Although some literature sources present an increasing focus on human factors (Smith et al., 2013; Joshi et al., 2020) and describe underestimated cultural and social issues as a key reason for failure (Cartwright and Schoenberg, 2006; Steigenberger, 2017), this was emphasised even more in the interviews. In 33 of 55 interviews related themes were addressed and included values like trust, respect, mindfulness, openness, eye-level and patience or principles like transparency, people focus, understanding, capacity, change and agility. Defining this set of soft aspects as common ground and as load-bearing ground in the visual framework visualises the importance of these critical success factors. Many similar reasons for failure in the literature (Tetenbaum, 1999; Jansen, 2016) as well as criticised process weaknesses during the interviews (see section 4.3, 4.5) can be led back to a lack of commitment to these joint values and principles, required as investment from both sides. Especially sufficient focus on capacity, change and agility were underlined as essential also during the focus group workshops.

In conclusion, these success factors demonstrate as synthesis of secondary and primary data evaluation, that underestimating or not properly considering them during an M&A project can lead to failure. Transferred back to the visual framework, this illustrates that if either the steps are not built properly or the columns are not built with equal strength or height or the ground under the building is not stable, the roof will collapse. As these components are backed up by both literature and practical experiences, their relevance is evident, however, prioritisation was pursued rather than completeness. This framework makes furthermore transparent that integration success has many prerequisites in the previous phases. The following section will elaborate further, how these success factors can be transferred to practice.

5.2 Process Framework—Transfer to Practice

Whilst the visual framework summarises key success factors, practical implementation and applicability require a transfer of these findings to the specific organisational context. Therefore, the consequent next development step was the analysis of the existing M&A process at D&S and the comparison to the previously elaborated success factors to identify necessary system interventions and improvement potentials. These measures were reflected in the focus groups and developed with detailed descriptions of every module. The created process overview aims for transparency and common understanding and illustrates which measures contribute to the steps of the visual building framework (Fig. 5.2). The combination of the general visual framework and the company-specific process framework allows readers and applicants to understand all required components, as the visual framework alone would lack a detailed transfer to practice, but adds the layer of values and principles. Important potential interventions are a systematic strategy workshop during the initiation phase, a holistic concept for the due diligence, integration planning workshops and an encompassing integration management system. These components are explained further in the following sections.

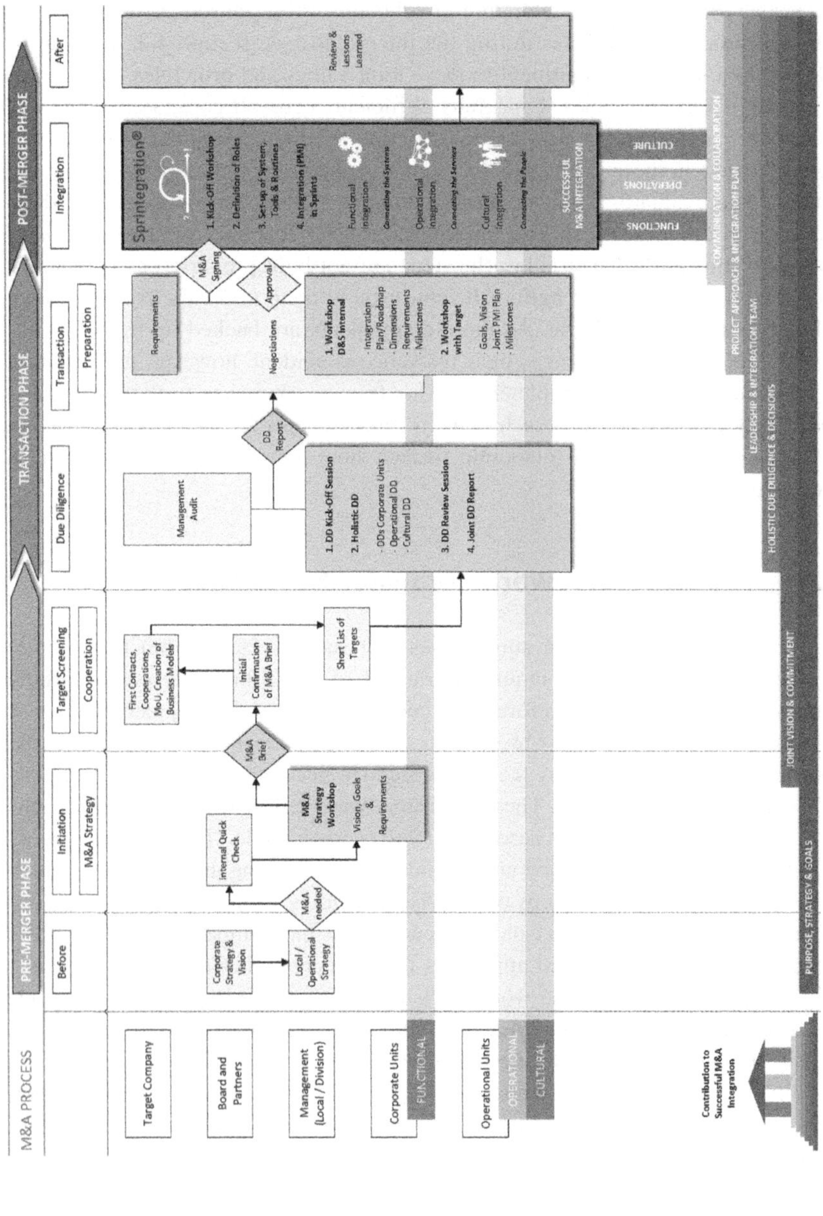

Fig. 5.2 Process Framework—M&A Process including potential Interventions

In 31 of 55 interviews the importance of a clear vision and strategy was highlighted, especially the consulted M&A consultants emphasised the creation of a consistent deal thesis (III.11, III.14) and the development of a vision and target organisation (III.8, III.12). This is supported by scholars like Gerds and Schewe (2014) or Meckl and Röhrle (2016) identifying strategy as basis for integration success and communication, however, contradicted by the description of the reality. 56% of the representatives of operative units mentioned a lack of vision and strategy in their M&A cases, supported by 50% of members of corporate units missing the big picture in addition to their individual tasks. Transferred to the M&A process, the elaboration of vision and strategy is anchored in the initiation phase, however, was partially skipped due to opportunistic decisions (I.1, I.4, I.15) or done without the involvement of all relevant stakeholders (I.14, I.19). These findings have led to the suggested intervention of a detailed M&A strategy workshop. Like all components, this workshop is conceptualised holistically including required participants, duration, suggested agenda, key topics, methods, workshop settings and guiding questions (Fig. 5.3). This level of detail allows a systematic implementation and provides the aspired applicability of this research. All details are based on requirements identified in interviews and literature and were furthermore validated regarding process architecture or workshop design with focus group I (process consultants). Key changes and interventions manifested in this strategy workshop are an early involvement of both the M&A representatives from the corporate units and the operative management (location or division) as well as the optional moderation through an M&A integration expert. The objectives of this workshop are strategy development, M&A target profile definition including selection criteria, project set-up according to the PMI knowledge areas (Patel, 2012) and an initial roadmap for the following steps. These results are summarised in an M&A brief, serving as basic information for all involved people in later stages to increase transparency.

For the due diligence phase the identified improvement potentials cover a Q&A session between the responsible management and all corporate units (II.5, II.8, III.10) which creates a joint understanding, involvement of operative management and experts for the evaluation of operational capabilities and cultural fit (II.12, I.12, I.22), a joint evaluation of all findings in a review session and a joint DD report (II.2, II.5). A holistic DD as key intervention covers beside functional and economical aspects also an operational and cultural analysis of the target organisation, inspired by literature sources like Dörrenbächer and Witzmann (2015) or Denison and Ko (2016). This extended DD concept is supported

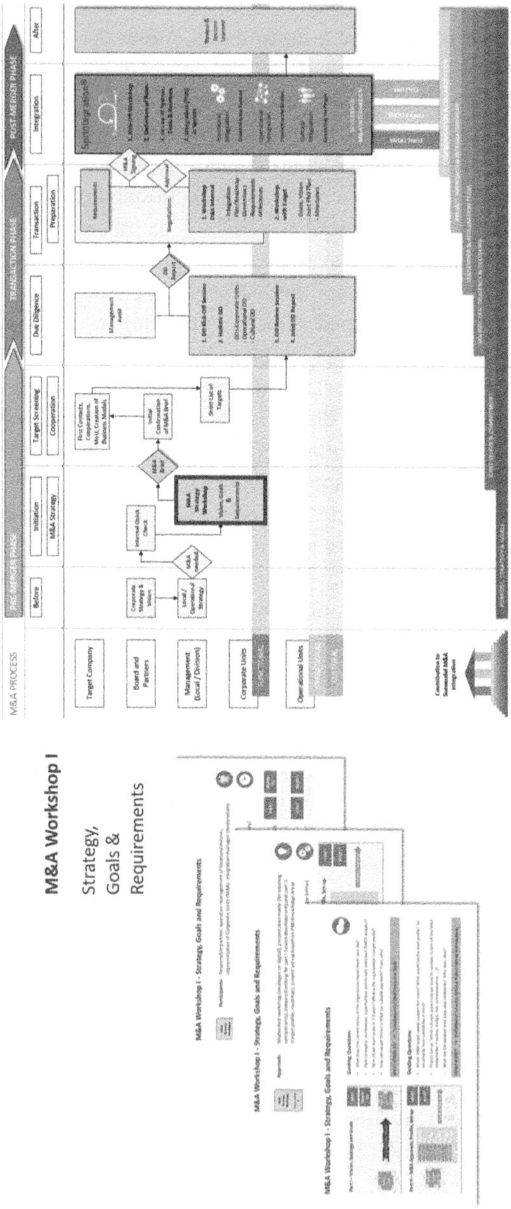

Fig. 5.3 M&A Strategy Workshop—Concept and Workshop Design

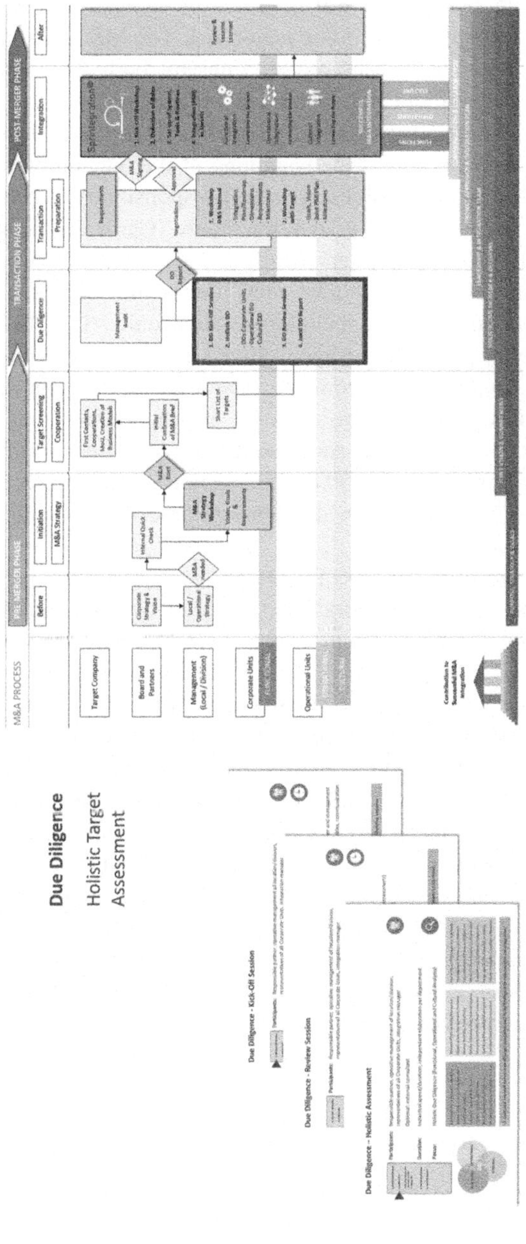

Fig. 5.4 Holistic Due Diligence—Concept and Collaboration Design

by scholars like Bischoff (2007), Hromei (2013) or Moeller and Brady (2014) who identified an incomplete DD as a major risk for M&A failure and can improve the collaboration and joint project thinking both between individual departments as well as corporate and operational units (Fig. 5.4). Remaining gaps due to informational asymmetry (Hromei, 2013; Patel, 2019) or lack of access (II.1, II.12) need to be addressed at the beginning of the integration phase.

Although several literature sources present a responsibility gap between the deal team and the integration team as risk for failure (Gerds and Schewe, 2014; Meynerts-Stiller, 2019), this is systematically avoided within D&S by having a consistent PMI team of the corporate units throughout DD and integration (II.1, II.12). However, it does not include operative units (II.2, II.4, II.5) and the withdraw of the strategic management after signing (Bergamin and Braun, 2018) is also evident within D&S (compare section 4.4). The joint development of an integration concept is therefore not only an important component in the literature (Venzin et al., 2018), but addresses also one of the priorities for the interview participants (mentioned in 39 of 55 interviews, compare section 4.6) for orientation and stability within the evident change process, to support employee retention and identification.

This was considered in the process framework by two workshops for integration preparation, first an internal workshop, followed by a second one together with the target representatives. Focus topics of these workshops, which are equally conceptualised in detail (Fig. 5.5), are the definition of integration areas, degree and speed based on theory models like the Culture End-State Framework (Denison and Ko, 2016, based on Marks and Mirvis, 1992, see section 2.3), the draft of the future organisation, key decisions regarding roles, a continuation of the project approach (Patel, 2012) and the commitment to goals and measurable success criteria. The latter integrates systematically the requirement of KPIs and performance measurement (Hromei, 2013; Jansen, 2016) and creates transparency about objectives to avoid diversity in success evaluation (compare section 4.5). Finally, an involvement of the target (Colombo et al., 2010; Lakshman, 2011) in the integration planning also contributes to the common ground of the visual framework and supports eye-level, understanding and trust while avoiding pure imposing of integration measures (mentioned in 33 of 55 interviews).

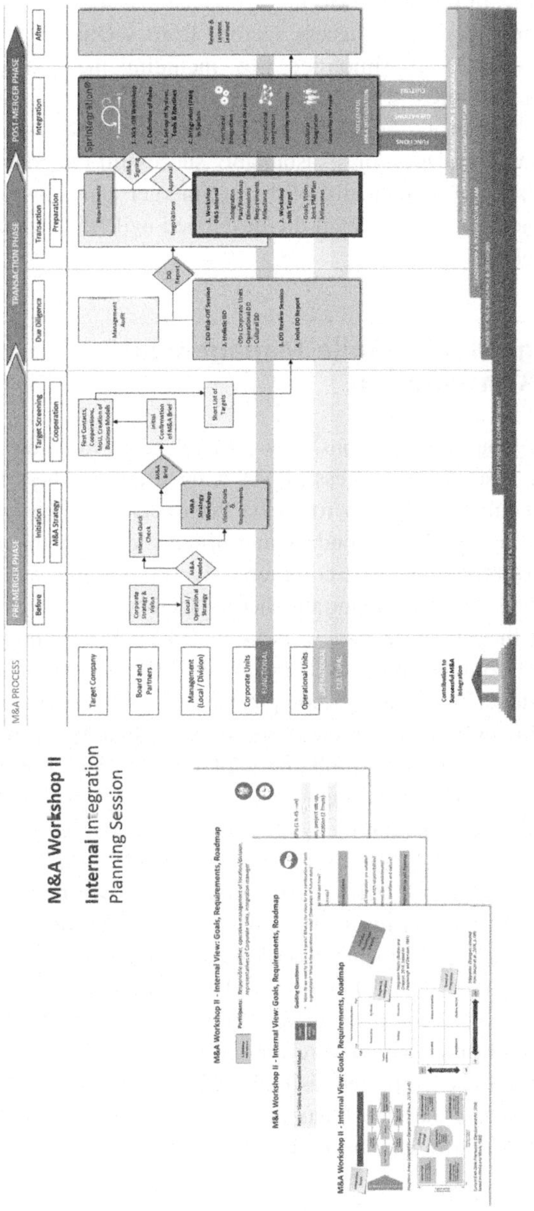

Fig. 5.5 Integration Preparation—Concept and Workshop Design

These interventions in this process framework enable a successful M&A integration by addressing identified success factors from secondary and primary data evaluation in a practical, simplified way including the detailed description of all required measures. This contributes to the planned applicability of all research results, enhances the mindset of continuous process improvement and contributes to the foundation of a sustainably successful integration by manifesting its prerequisites systematically in the pre-merger and transaction phase. The following chapter presents in detail the developed agile management system for the integration phase.

5.3 Sprintegration®—Agile Management for M&A Integration

Building on the previous interventions, this research aims for the development of a framework for sustainably successful M&A integration, which has besides the elaborated prerequisites its main focus on the integration phase. Therefore, all identified requirements from secondary and primary data for this phase were combined and prioritised to create a comprehensive system that can be applied in real cases, covering the most important success factors.

As identified in the literature review (section 2.4.1), M&A integrations are highly dynamic and complex projects (Engelhardt 2017; Bergamin and Braun, 2018; Meynerts-Stiller, 2019), due to complexity factors like dynamic environment, duration, number of stakeholders, speed or ambiguity of requirements (Poveda-Bautista et al., 2018) or probability of changes and low predictability (Sohi et al., 2016). This was supported especially by the external M&A experts describing the combination of two social systems as highly dynamic and unplannable (III.6, III.8), also based on a lack of complete information due to limitations of the due diligence (III.13). This high complexity requires a project management approach that can react to changes (compare section 2.4.3), which is backed up by interview participants describing a required approach as adaptive (I.2, I.7, I.10) or agile (I.29, II.8, II.11). Patel (2019) identified that in practice this complexity is often addressed with methods that are rather suitable for a complicated or simple context and has therefore created his work on Agile M&A. This perspective can partially be supported, as both within D&S and in external cases traditional PM approaches like checklists or linear schedules (I.3, II.1, III.5) are applied, but the M&A consultants have provided valuable impulses for agility in

M&As (III.12, III.13), even arguing that they have always managed the integration in agile ways (III.14). However, except Patel's work there is little guidance on the implementation of an agile M&A system.

This led to the decision to develop an agile integration management system, which allows adaptation to change, enhances collaboration and communication, addresses the challenges holistically (functional, operational and cultural integration), establishes all required roles and allows an integration in time-boxed sprints including the ability to reflect, react and learn. The created brand Sprintegration® (Fig. 5.6) combines the integration aim with the Scrum method and consists of six areas, which cover a holistic view on all identified success factors:

- Vision & Strategy
- Set-up & Processes
- Roles & Organisation
- Events & Routines
- Tools & Systems
- Lessons Learned

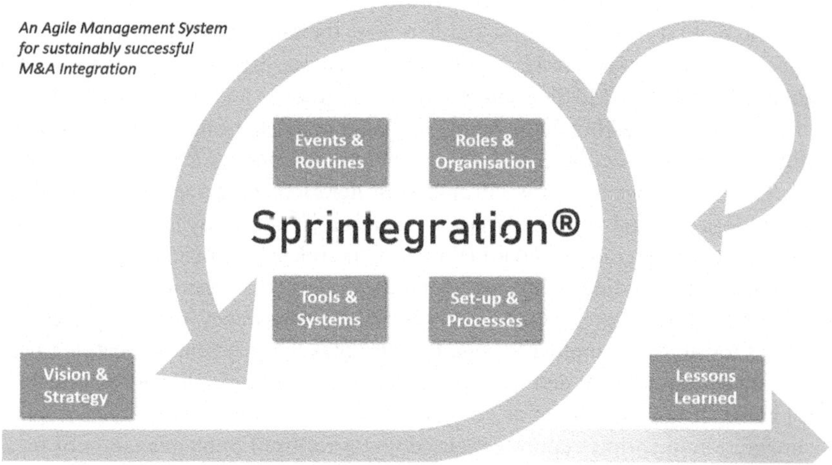

Fig. 5.6 Sprintegration®—Agile Management System for M&A Integration

These six core areas are broken down into 36 individual modules (see Fig. 5.7), which are developed in detail including descriptions of input, process, output and contributors. This level of detail as continuation of the process framework components supports completeness and applicability. The following sections summarize and describe prioritised modules as examples.

Sprintegration® sets up an agile project under consideration of all identified required roles (Fig. 5.8). The decision level, described as crucial during the interviews (I.4, I.12, II.9), supported by several scholars (Bergamin and Braun, 2018; Meynerts-Stiller, 2019), is formed by a steering committee from both organisations. The project is led by a dedicated integration manager (Trichterborn et al., 2015), whose profile is covering criteria discussed in the interviews like experience within the acquiring company, strong identification and network, operational background, method and communication skills and required capacity (mentioned in 23 interviews), in accordance with Gerds and Schewe (2014) or Moeller and Brady (2014) as elaborated in section 2.3.3. Furthermore, the integration team consists of representatives from both organisations for all relevant workstreams (Stankiewicz-Mróz, 2015; Sherman, 2018) who also act as promoters towards their teams (Bergamin and Braun, 2018). The workstreams cover besides all functional corporate units also the operational and cultural integration, which brings to life the one company thinking (I.1, II.1, II.12) and a holistic approach for M&A integration (I.3, I.20, II.3). Furthermore, the currently low involvement of external expertise (compare section 4.4) is increased, especially for the required change management (Moeller and Brady, 2014; Rebner and Yeganeh, 2019).

This team is working in a highly collaborative environment based on the Scrum method (see section 2.4.3). A joint integration plan as a key success factor (addressed in 39 interviews) is developed in iterations based on the workstream goals, milestones and prioritised tasks. Therefore, both a physical and a virtual version of a Sprintegration® board (Fig. 5.9) and related events and routines were conceptualised including templates, methods and process descriptions.

This allows local presence in the office and transparency regarding progress and roles towards the employees, which contributes to open communication (mentioned in 29 interviews), and a virtual collaboration in cross-border acquisitions (Erel et al., 2012; Boateng et al., 2019).

Integration in sprints supports focused and prioritised implementation of measures, close learning and adjustment loops, iterations and focus on the vision and contributes to integration through collaboration on eye-level. Changes can be dealt with in every sprint planning through new priorities or milestones and the

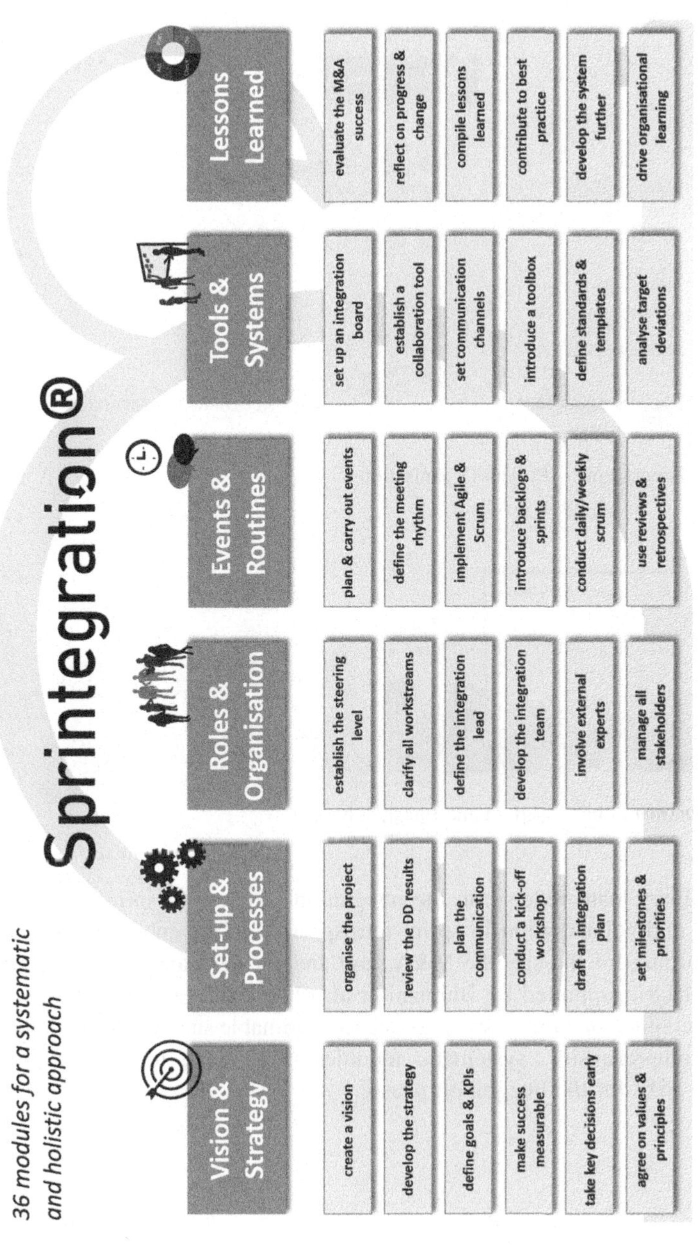

Fig. 5.7 Sprintegration®—Overview 36 Modules

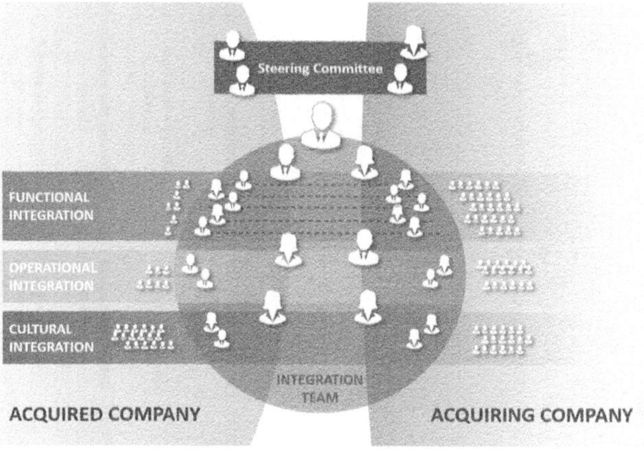

Fig. 5.8 Sprintegration®—Project Organisation

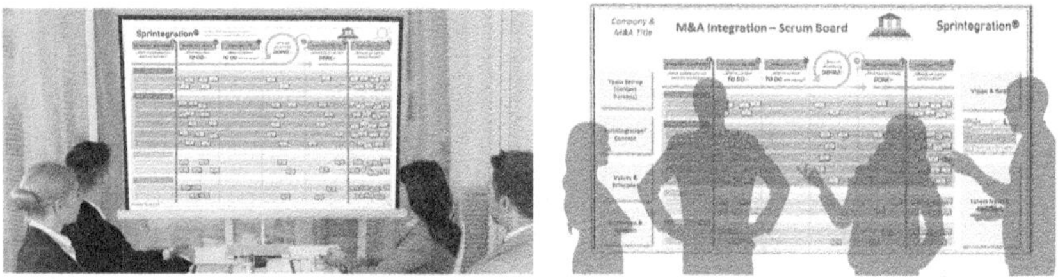

Fig. 5.9 Sprintegration®—Virtual and Physical Boards

interdisciplinary team reflects on the integration progress in sprint reviews and on process and collaboration in sprint retrospectives. This enhances the organisational learning for the specific M&A case and for the transfer to future cases (II.1, II.7, III.8), supported by Bhimani et al. (2015) and Hečková et al. (2019) describing continuous improvement as key to sustainable success. Sprintegration® provides comprehensive, systematic modules (Fig. 5.10) to address success factors and risks for the integration phase.

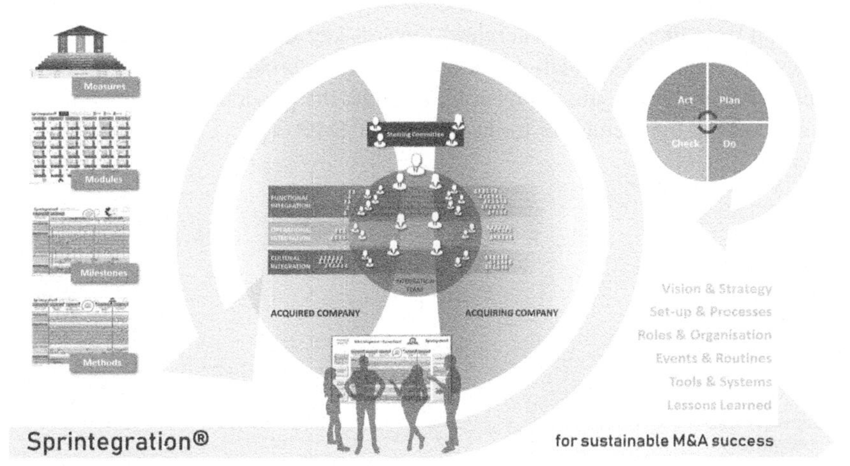

Fig. 5.10 Sprintegration®—System Overview

5.4 Summary

The evaluation of secondary and primary data on successful M&A integration demonstrated a high accordance of findings. Similarities in topics like strategy, roles, collaboration, joint plans, transparency, communication, external expertise or agility and adaptability reinforced their definition as key success factors. Minor controversial opinions or contradictions regarding the impact of size, distance and culture were already evident in the literature and underlined in the interviews, however, the detailed primary data shed light on the importance of these aspects in international organisations with smaller M&As and strong people focus. Furthermore, the interviews added more precise layers of learnings and requirements which allowed the development of a tailor-made system and specific interventions. The focus groups contributed to the applicability through detailed feedback on process architecture, workshop designs and the transfer to the D&S context. Overall, the decision for an agile integration system was based on high complexity and the aim to enhance collaboration as a natural measure for operational and cultural integration. Although no system can define personal behaviour, the application of Scrum methods fosters communication, transparency, openness, reflection, eye-level and learning and thereby contributes with an inherent set of values and principles to the common ground of human factors in M&As.

This system was developed based on a stringent approach of data complexity reduction from literature and interviews towards key success factors and the visual framework (Fig. 5.11), which was afterwards again broken down and detailed to assure its applicability, always measured against the previously identified success factors and the transferability to the context of D&S.

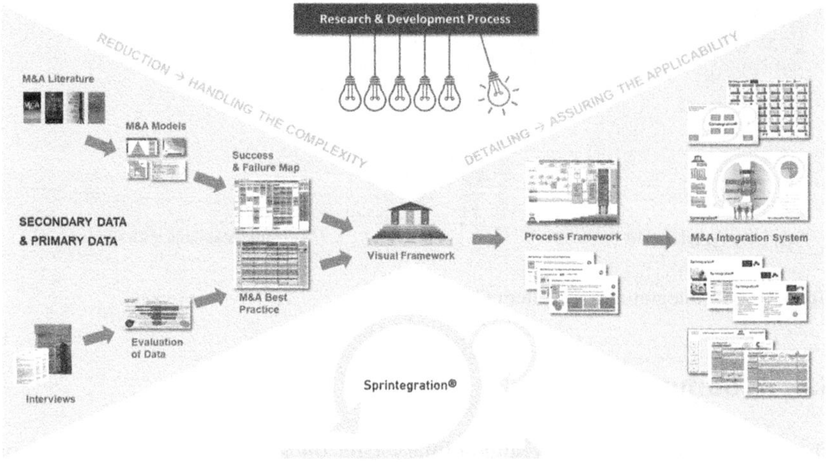

Fig. 5.11 Research and Development Process

6 Conclusion

6.1 General Conclusion

This research was undertaken to identify measures and methods which mitigate the risk of failure of M&A integration. The definition of M&As as projects led to the research question:

How can a project management approach lead to a sustainably successful post-merger integration within an international real estate enterprise?

The literature review regarding theoretical background, definitions, statistics, reasons for failure or success and integration management approaches covered the research objectives 1 and 2. The primary data collected through 55 interviews with internal and external participants (research objective 3) completed the basis by adding the specific company context, different stakeholder perspectives, previous M&A experiences and external expertise.

As this study aims for high applicability of all results to address a practical problem and improve professional practice, consequently the research objective 4 strived for synthesising these findings in a project management framework as key result to achieve the overall research aim. Quality and applicability were furthermore reinforced through the framework verification in two focus groups with experts.

It can be concluded that all research objectives as well as the research aim of creating a framework for M&A integration with a high degree of applicability were achieved (Fig. 6.1, details in Table 6.1).

M. Miller, *Sprintegration®—An Agile Framework for M&A Integration*, BestMasters, https://doi.org/10.1007/978-3-658-37455-6_6

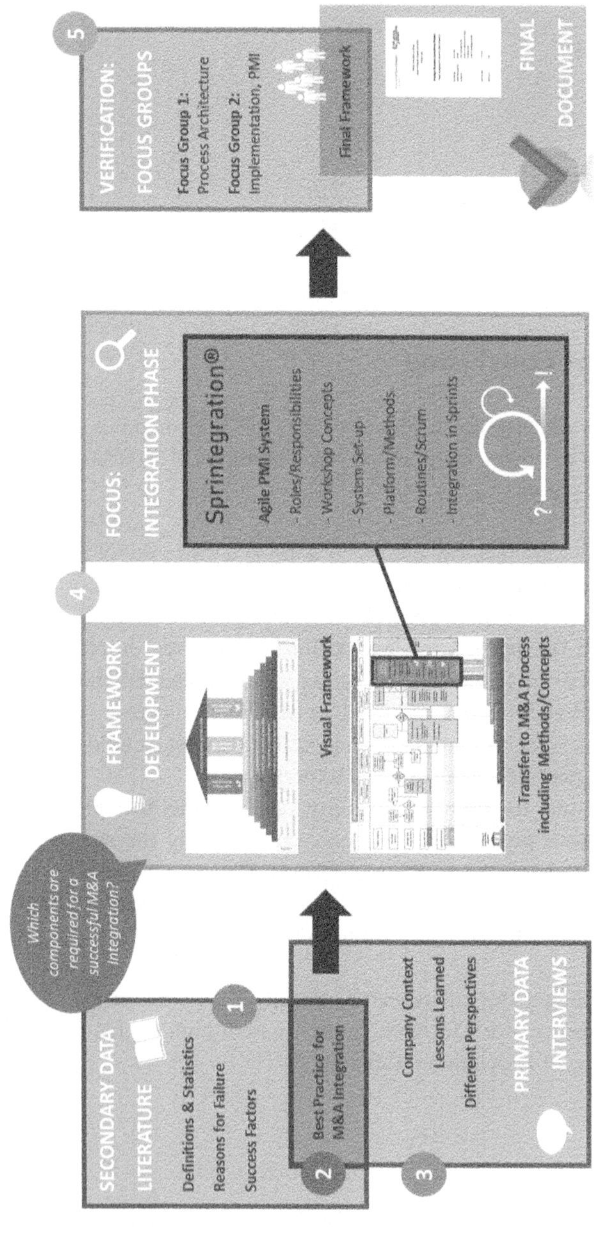

Fig. 6.1 Overview Research Objectives and Results

Table 6.1 Research Objectives—Evaluation

	Research Objectives	Evaluation and Conclusion
1	To systematically identify and synthesize success factors and failure criteria for M&A in literature	Achieved through detailed and critical integrative literature review and synthesis of findings in Success & Failure Map
2	To critically analyse M&A best practice in theory and practice, with focus on integration management and its prerequisites	Achieved through encompassing literature review and evaluation of interviews, especially of the external experts
3	To comprehensively investigate 12 M&A cases at D&S regarding context and lessons learned	Achieved through 55 interviews (41 internal, 14 external) and systematic data analysis
4	To design and develop a project management framework for M&A integration including applicable methods and tools	Achieved through synthesis of findings from secondary and primary data, transfer to company context and detailed creation of an applicable system (Sprintegration®)
5	To critically appraise and verify the project management framework in two focus groups	Achieved through focus group 1 (internal and external process consultants) and focus group 2 (internal M&A team of corporate units) and the integration of their feedback

Based on this elaboration, the research question can be answered as follows: Due to the evident high complexity of M&A projects, agile management approaches are required as they allow adaptation of plans to an unpredictable and changing environment, enhance collaboration and create the value and synergies, which were the original M&A decision drivers, in transparent iterations. Therefore, key success factors and the agile method of Scrum were combined in the systematic and comprehensive integration framework Sprintegration®. Furthermore, the sustainability addressed in the research question depends on holistic approaches during due diligence and integration, covering functional, operational and cultural aspects and a common ground of joint values and principles. As this study responds to a challenge in the real business context as a strategic business consultancy project, the transferability and connectivity to the organisational processes had a high priority. According to the focus groups, especially the detailed development of individual process components and interventions allows their future implementation. In conclusion, for an international real estate company with strong focus on people and their knowledge, an environment for collaboration and communication with transparent measures based on joint and conscious integration decisions can support employee retention and an agile, collaborative approach can contribute naturally to operational and cultural understanding and a joint focus on creating the pursued synergies. Sprintegration® manifests these success factors in roles, routines, tools and methods, contributing eventually to continuous improvement and organisational learning. This closes the circle to sustainable success in M&A integration and organisational practice.

The research paradigm of pragmatism and the related research methodology have proven to be effective, as they focused the study on solving a real practical problem through applied research and emphasis on research problem and context. The inductive, qualitative and exploratory approach has enabled a rich data basis, a deep exploration of a highly complex topic and the creation of a contribution to the world of knowledge that can be further tested and developed in practice. Qualitative research was very valuable, as many significant findings evolved from open dialogue and deepening questions. M&A integration is connected to very personal and intimate experiences and required a high attention on ethics and the creation of trust. Especially the interviews have underpinned the importance to focus on this subject and reinforced and enriched the framework creation. Thematic analysis through the method of template analysis enabled not only the examination of the very rich primary data, but was as a concept also transferred to the literature review by identifying key themes and a priori themes throughout the whole study. This approach was essential to create transparency, to reduce complexity and to identify the key criteria as framework components.

As described in section 1.4, this research had a clear focus on a specific segment of the wide context of M&A, which naturally leads to limitations. The research focused on friendly M&As with smaller sizes in a people focused service field, so applicability for different M&A scenarios or transferability to other industries is not automatically given. Although the purposive sampling included a high number of interview participants and external experts, organisational transformation and the associated experiences are highly subjective and even a high number of results can only provide an indication, but no transferable truth. Furthermore, the scope of this study restricted a deeper testing or examination in practice, which is planned in the future, but not covered within this research. The developed framework does consciously not cover individual defined measures for functional, operational or cultural integration as they require tailor-made decisions in every specific case, however, aims for providing a framework that enables the elaboration and joint decision of these measures. The feedback from experts and the high accordance with general findings in the literature could suggest a transferability to other organisations, nevertheless, all components would need to be reflected, questioned and adapted to the specific context. Finally, throughout the research project, prioritisation was pursued rather than completeness. The identified success factors, integrated in the visual framework, are based on this specific research and the related findings, other researchers might come to different conclusions.

These limitations also lead to recommendations for further research. Especially a cross-border context and virtual connection could benefit from further research on how the success of M&As depends on personal contact and collaboration in real life and if agile systems like Sprintegration® can have an evident impact.

As raised by Brueller et al. (2014), who state that M&As could even facilitate strategic and organisational agility, another recommendation would be a research on how agility in M&A integration impacts the overall agility of companies. In addition, the difference between industries and organisations which already have implemented agile methods, for example IT development companies, and more traditional companies like within the construction sector, in the acceptance and success of agile integration methods could be investigated. Finally, also a study on holistic due diligence approaches could increase the knowledge in this area, as most studies have a specific focus on only one area.

This research contributes to organisational development and professional practice of D&S through transparency about previous cases and external best practice. The process implementation is currently strategically discussed. Although the level of detail supports the applicability, the research has also shed light on hinderances like budget and capacity, cultural components like profit focus and priority for operational business or the heterogeneity of cases and responsibilities, which demonstrate that systematic interventions and investments are required to reinforce future M&A success, that roles need to be developed and that leadership skills in complex change situations cannot be delegated or compensated by a system.

6.2 Personal Reflection

My personal reflection of the development throughout this research leads first to an evaluation of the SWOT analysis undertaken during the research proposal stage. Its purpose was to critically assess personal abilities, opportunities and threats for the research success in the organisational context (Fig. 6.2). Whilst I could in fact benefit from my strong internal network, the communication, listening and structuring skills and the previous M&A experiences, anticipated weaknesses like a lack of distance or the double role through insider research were handled with high awareness which avoided conflicts. The risk of lack of experience in research of this scope could meanwhile be transformed to solid confidence in handling research projects with high amount of qualitative data. The opportunities have not changed in general, however the Corona crisis impacted the investments. Although the threats of little appreciation for internal development or resistance from internal experts could be avoided through open and transparent communication, the limited capacities might also in the future stay a challenge. The exercise of applying a SWOT analysis to a research project was very helpful for me to keep the key factors in mind. This research has equipped me with expert knowledge that I can apply in my role as Head of international TQM and in future M&A cases and can therefore personally be seen as very successful.

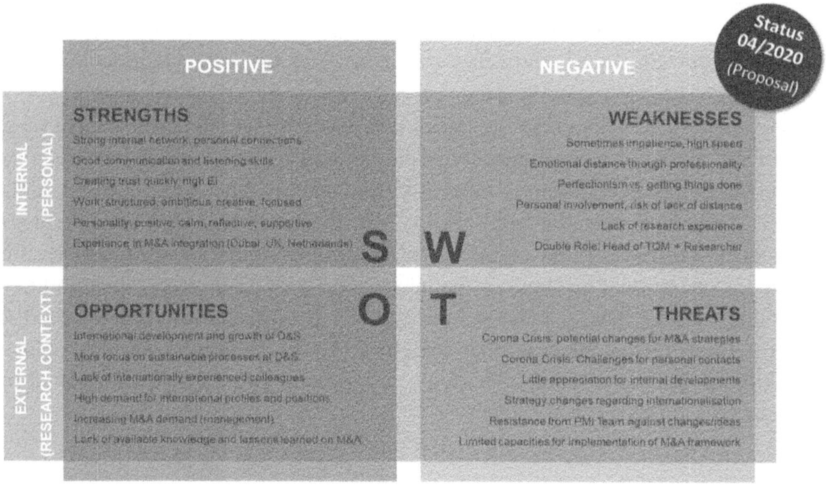

Fig. 6.2 SWOT Analysis, Status: Proposal

Overall, I can conclude that the deep investigation and development of agile methods in the context of a year dominated by Covid19 provided me with a very encompassing experience of agility. Therefore, a second interpretation of M&A besides mergers and acquisitions is properly summarising the phase and learnings of this research: **M**yself **&** **A**gility (Fig. 6.3).

The personal life required high agility to deal with new restrictions, low predictability and continuous change of plans, whilst the Corona crisis also changed the work life regarding mobility, home office and more virtual business. The personal behaviour changed very fast and individual or organisational agility were key factors for maintaining success and positivity.

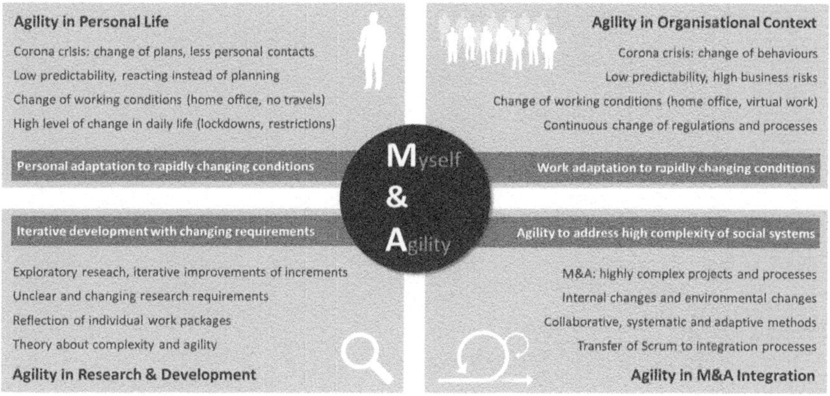

Fig. 6.3 Personal Reflection

Furthermore, agility was not only the identified best approach for M&A to deal with the complexity of social systems, but also applied and experienced throughout the whole research progress, including exploratory, collaborative development and iterative creation of all results. This research project has deeply enriched my personal knowledge and awareness about agility and indirectly supported me to deal with the research itself in a challenging external and personal context. It has therefore contributed not only to professional development and learning, but also to personal skill development and embracing of change.

References

Abdou, S.M., Yong, K. and Othman, M., (2016) Project Complexity Influence on Project management performance-The Malaysian perspective. *MATEC Web of Conferences*, 66. DOI: https://doi.org/10.1051/matecconf/20166600065.

Achtenhagen, L., Brunninge, O. and Melin, L., (2017) Patterns of Dynamic Growth in Medium-Sized Companies: Beyond the Dichotomy of Organic Versus Acquired Growth. *Long Range Planning*, [online] 504, pp. 457–471. DOI: http://dx.doi.org/10.1016/j.lrp.2016.08.003.

Ahammad, M.F. and Glaister, K.W., (2011) Postacquisition management and performance of cross-border acquisitions. *International Studies of Management and Organization*, 413, pp. 59–75. DOI: https://doi.org/10.2753/IMO0020-8825410304.

Ahammad, M.F., Tarba, S.Y., Liu, Y. and Glaister, K.W., (2016) Knowledge transfer and cross-border acquisition performance: The impact of cultural distance and employee retention. *International Business Review*, [online] 251, pp. 66–75. DOI: http://dx.doi.org/10.1016/j.ibusrev.2014.06.015.

Alami, A., (2015) Can Agile Reduce Complexity? *Project Smart*. pp. 1–4. Available at: https://www.projectsmart.co.uk/pdf/can-agile-reduce-complexity.pdf [Accessed 29 Oct. 2020].

Anderson, H., Havila, V. and Nilsson, F., (2012) Mergers and acquisitions: The critical role of stakeholders. *Mergers and Acquisitions:The Critical Role of Stakeholders*, February, pp. 1–289. DOI: https://doi.org/10.4324/9780203111376.

Azan, W. and Huber Sutter, I., (2010) Knowledge transfer in post-merger integration management: Case study of a multinational healthcare company in Greece. *Knowledge Management Research and Practice*, [online] 84, pp. 307–321. DOI: http://dx.doi.org/10.1057/kmrp.2010.17.

Baird, L., Harding, D., Horsley, P. and Dhar, S., (2019) M&A in Disruption: 2018 in Review. *Bain & Company*. [online] Available at: https://www.bain.com/insights/M-and-A-in-disruption-2018-in-review/. [Accessed 09 Oct. 2020].

Beck, K., Grenning, J., Martin, R., Beedle, M., Highsmith, J. and Mellor, S., (2001) Manifesto for Agile Software Development. *The Agile Alliance*, [online] pp. 12–14. Available at: http://agilemanifesto.org/. [Accessed 05 Nov. 2020].

M. Miller, *Sprintegration®—An Agile Framework for M&A Integration*, BestMasters, https://doi.org/10.1007/978-3-658-37455-6

Bergamin, S. and Braun, M., (2018) Mergers and acquisitions: Integration and Transformation Management as the Gateway to Success. Springer. DOI: https://doi.org/10.1007/978-3-319-60504-3.

Bhimani, A., Ncube, M. and Sivabalan, P., (2015) Managing risk in mergers and acquisitions activity: Beyond 'good' and 'bad' management. *Managerial Auditing Journal*, 302, pp. 160–175. DOI: https://doi.org/10.1108/MAJ-08-2014-1079.

Bischoff J.M. (2007) Change Management in M&A-Projekten – Von der Cultural Due Diligence zur Post-Merger-Integration. In: Nachhaltiges Change Management. Gabler. DOI: https://doi.org/10.1007/978-3-8349-9531-5_3.

Boateng, A., Du, M., Bi, X.G. and Lodorfos, G., (2019) Cultural distance and value creation of cross-border M&A: The moderating role of acquirer characteristics. *International Review of Financial Analysis*, [online] 63December 2018, pp. 285–295. DOI: https://doi.org/10.1016/j.irfa.2018.12.009.

Bodner, J. and Capron, L., (2018) Post-merger Integration. *Journal of Organization Design, Springer*; Organizational Design Community, vol.7(1), pp. 1–9. DOI: https://doi.org/10.1186/s41469-018-0027-4.

Bouwman, C.H.S., (2013) The role of corporate culture in mergers and acquisitions. *Mergers and Acquisitions Practices, Performance and Perspectives*, May, pp. 109–131. Available at: https://mba.americaeconomia.com/sites/mba.americaeconomia.com/files/paper_2.pdf [Accessed 09 Oct. 2020].

Brekke, K.R., Siciliani, L. and Straume, O.R., (2017) Horizontal mergers and product quality. *Canadian Journal of Economics*, 504, pp. 1063–1103. DOI: https://doi.org/10.1111/caje.12287.

Bristow, A. and Saunders, M., (2014) Heightening awareness of research philosophy: the development of a reflexive tool for use with students. *British Academy of Management (BAM) 2014 Conference Proceedings*, pp. 2–11. Available at: https://www.bl.uk/britishlibrary/~/media/bl/global/business-and-management/pdfs/non-secure/h/e/i/heightening-awareness-of-research-philosophy-the-development-of-a-reflexive-tool-for-use-with-students.pdf [Accessed 25 Oct. 2020].

Britten, N., (2007) Qualitative Interviews. In: *Qualitative Research in Health Care: Third Edition*. DOI: https://doi.org/10.1002/9780470750841.ch2.

Brooks, J. and King, N., (2014) Doing Template Analysis: Evaluating an End-of-Life Care Service. *Doing Template Analysis: Evaluating an End-of-Life Care Service*, March. DOI: https://dx.doi.org/10.4135/978144627305013512755.

Brueller, N.N., Carmeli, A. and Drori, I., (2014) How do different types of mergers and acquisitions facilitate strategic agility? *California Management Review*, 563, pp. 39–57. DOI: https://dx.doi.org/10.1525/cmr.2014.56.3.39.

Bruni-Bossio, V., Sheehan, N.T. and Willness, C.R., (2018) Circle mapping your firm's growth strategy. *Business Horizons*, [online] 612, pp. 285–296. DOI: http://dx.doi.org/10.1016/j.bushor.2017.11.010.

Buschmann, H., (2019) M & A-Trends für Strategen. pp. 18–23. *Forum Mergers & Acquisitions 2019*. Beiträge aus rechts- und wirtschaftswissenschaftlicher Sicht, Wiesbaden. Available at: www.springerprofessional.de/link/16788738 [Accessed 05 Oct. 2020].

Cartwright, S. and Schoenberg, R., (2006) Thirty years of mergers and acquisitions research: Recent advances and future opportunities. *British Journal of Management*. DOI: https://dx.doi.org/10.1111/j.1467-8551.2006.00475.x.

Cervone, H.F., (2011) Understanding agile project management methods using Scrum. *OCLC Systems and Services*, 271, pp. 18–22. DOI: https://dx.doi.org/10.1108/10650751111106528.

Charoensukmongkol, P., (2017) Contributions of mindfulness during post-merger integration. *Journal of Managerial Psychology*, 321, pp. 104–118. DOI: https://dx.doi.org/10.1108/JMP-02-2016-0039.

Cheek, B., (2016) The Stacey matrix. [online] Available at: http://www.gp-training.net/training/communication_skills/consultation/equipoise/complexity/stacey.htm. [Accessed 15 Nov. 2020].

Christensen, C.M., Alton, R., Rising, C. and Waldeck, A., (2011) The New M & A Playbook. *Harvard business review*, [online] March, pp. 1–11. Available at: https://hbr.org/2011/03/the-big-idea-the-new-ma-playbook. [Accessed 08 Oct. 2020].

Colombo, L., Cusumano, T., Duarte, C., Baral, D., Pollak, S. and Suidan, M., (2010) Talking about the people side of M&A. *PwC*. [online] Available at: https://www.pwc.co.uk/assets/pdf/talking-about-the-people-side-of-m-and-a.pdf [Accessed 17 Oct. 2020].

Connaughton, J., Meikle, J. and Teerikangas, S., (2015) Mergers, acquisitions and the evolution of construction professional services firms. *Construction Management and Economics*, [online] 332, pp. 146–159. DOI: http://dx.doi.org/10.1080/01446193.2015.1037325.

Cooper, D.R. and Schindler, P.S., (2014) *Business Research Methods 12th Edition. Business Research Methods*. New York: McGraw-Hill.

Cotei, C. and Farhat, J., (2018) The M&A exit outcomes of new, young firms. *Small Business Economics*, 503, pp. 545–567. DOI: http://dx.doi.org/10.1007/s11187-017-9907-1.

Cristóbal, J.R.S., (2017) Complexity in Project Management. *Procedia Computer Science*, 121, pp. 762–766. DOI: https://doi.org/10.1016/j.procs.2017.11.098.

Degbey, W.Y., Rodgers, P., Kromah, M.D. and Weber, Y., (2020) The impact of psychological ownership on employee retention in mergers and acquisitions. *Human Resource Management Review*, [online] p.100745. DOI https://doi.org/10.1016/j.hrmr.2020.100745.

Denison, D.R. and Ko, I., (2016) Cultural due diligence in mergers and acquisitions. *Advances in Mergers and Acquisitions*, 15July 2016, pp. 53–72. DOI: https://doi.org/10.1108/S1479-361X20160000015004.

Denning, S., (2019) Lessons learned from mapping successful and unsuccessful agile transformation journeys. *Strategy and Leadership*, 474, pp. 3–11. DOI: http://dx.doi.org/10.1108/SL-04-2019-0052.

Dorling, J.L., (2017) Impact of psychological capital on the resistance to change during post-merger integration: A theoretical model. *Journal of Organizational Change Management*, 306, pp. 936–956. DOI: http://dx.doi.org/10.1108/JOCM-11-2015-0199

Dörrenbächer, C. and Witzmann, N., (2015) The Link Between Cultural Due Diligence and Socio-Cultural Postmerger Integration Management as a Critical Success Factor in M&As. *Working Paper of the Insitute of Management Berlin at the Berlin Schoool of Economics and Law (HWR Berlin)*, 84, pp. 2–24. Available at: http://hdl.handle.net/10419/111286. [Accessed 19 Nov. 2020].

Dougherty, M.R., Slevc, L.R. and Grand, J.A., (2019) Making Research Evaluation More Transparent: Aligning Research Philosophy, Institutional Values, and Reporting. *Perspectives on Psychological Science*, 143, pp. 361–375. DOI: https://doi.org/10.1177/1745691618810693

www.dreso.com. (n.d.). *Drees & Sommer*. [online] Available at: https://www.dreso.com/de/ [Accessed 11 Nov. 2020].

Drees & Sommer, (2019) Annual Report 2018. Drees & Sommer, 41, pp. 1–179. Available at: https://www.dreso.com/en/jahresberichte/annual-report-2018/ [Accessed 11 Nov. 2020].

Drees & Sommer, (2018) Vision 2025, internal brochure (confidential), pp. 3–64

Durand, M., (2016) Employing critical incident technique as one way to display the hidden aspects of post-merger integration. *International Business Review*, [online] 251, pp. 87–102. Available at: http://dx.doi.org/10.1016/j.ibusrev.2015.05.003.

Duvall-Dickson, S., Dickson, K., Hoover, S., Jones, B.T., Maher, D. and Short, G., (2016) Blending Tribes : Leadership Challenges in Mergers and Acquisitions. pp. 16–23. Quarterly Journal. S.A.M. Advanced Management Journal, 81(4), pp. 16–22, 36. Available at: https://search.proquest.com/docview/1891317812/5D544229A2E945D3PQ/1?accountid=12118. [Accessed 16 Nov. 2020].

Easterby-Smith, M., Thorpe, R. and Jackson, P.R., (2018) *Management & business research.* Los Angeles, Calif.: SAGE.

Elliott, V., (2018) Thinking about the coding process in qualitative data analysis. *Qualitative Report*, 2311, pp. 2850–2861. Available at: https://nsuworks.nova.edu/tqr/vol23/iss11/14. [Accessed 16 Dec. 2020].

Engelhardt, C., (2017) Mergers & Acquisitions – Ablauf und Grundbegriffe im M&A-Geschäft. Springer: Wiesbaden. DOI http://dx.doi.org/10.1007/978-3-658-17066-0_2

Erel, I., Liao, R.C. and Weisbach, M.S., (2012) Determinants of Cross-Border Mergers and Acquisitions. *Journal of Finance*, 673, pp. 1045–1082. DOI: https://doi.org/10.1111/j.1540-6261.2012.01741.x.

EYGM Limited, (2019) M & A sector outlook 2019. *Ernst & Young Report 2019.* EYGM Limited.

Ficery, K., Herd, T. and Pursche, B., (2007) Where has all the synergy gone? the M&A puzzle. *Journal of Business Strategy*, 285, pp. 29–35. DOI: https://doi.org/10.1108/02756660710820802.

Filipović, D., (2012) Impact of company's size on takeover success. *Ekonomska Istrazivanja*, 252, pp. 435–444. DOI: https://doi.org/10.1080/1331677X.2012.11517516.

Finefter-Rosenbluh, I., (2017) Incorporating perspective taking in reflexivity: A method to enhance insider qualitative research processes. *International Journal of Qualitative Methods*, 161, pp. 1–11. DOI: https://doi.org/10.1177/1609406917703539

Fiorentino, R. and Garzella, S., (2015) Synergy management pitfalls in mergers and acquisitions. *Management Decision*, 537, pp. 1469–1503. DOI: https://doi.org/10.1108/MD-12-2014-0692

Florczak, K.L., (2017) Adding to the Truth of the Matter: The Case for Qualitative Research. *Nursing Science Quarterly*, 304, pp. 296–299. DOI: https://doi.org/10.1177/0894318417724466

Foss, N.J. and Saebi, T., (2018) Business models and business model innovation: Between wicked and paradigmatic problems. *Long Range Planning*, [online] 511, pp. 9–21. DOI: https://doi.org/10.1016/j.lrp.2017.07.006.

Friedman, Y., Carmeli, A., Tishler, A. and Shimizu, K., (2016) Untangling micro-behavioral sources of failure in mergers and acquisitions: a theoretical integration and extension. *International Journal of Human Resource Management*, [online] 2720, pp. 2339–2369. DOI: http://dx.doi.org/10.1080/09585192.2015.1042003.

Fu, F.Q., Phillips, J.J. and Phillips, P.P., (2018) ROI Marketing: Measuring, Demonstrating, and Improving Value. *Performance Improvement*, 572, pp. 6–13. DOI: https://doi.org/10.1002/pfi.21771

Gerds, J. and Schewe, G., (2014) Integration Excellence – Mit Fusionen und Akquisitionen zum Unternehmenserfolg. In: *Post Merger Integration*. Springer Gabler: Berlin.

Gill, P., Stewart, K., Treasure, E. and Chadwick, B., (2008) Methods of data collection in qualitative research: Interviews and focus groups. *British Dental Journal*. DOI: https://doi.org/10.1038/bdj.2008.192.

Grimpe, C. and Hussinger, K., (2007) Discussion Paper No. 07–066: Firm Acquisitions and Technology Strategy—Corporate versus Private Equity Investors. *Centre for European Economic Research*, [online] 07. Available at: http://ftp.zew.de/pub/zew-docs/dp/dp07066.pdf. [Accessed 16 Oct. 2020].

Gustafsson, J., (2017) Single case studies vs. multiple case studies: A comparative study. *Academy of Business, Engineering and Science Halmstad University, Sweden*, [online] pp. 1–15. Available at: https://www.diva-portal.org/smash/get/diva2:1064378/FULLTEXT01.pdf [Accessed 13 Dec. 2020].

Hannah, D.R. and Lautsch, B.A., (2011) Counting in qualitative research: Why to conduct it, when to avoid it, and when to closet it. *Journal of Management Inquiry*, 201, pp. 14–22. DOI: https://doi.org/10.1177/1056492610375988.

Hečková, J., Štefko, R., Frankovský, M., Birknerová, Z., Chapčáková, A. and Zbihlejová, L., (2019) Cross-border mergers and acquisitions as a challenge for sustainable business. *Sustainability (Switzerland)*, 1111, pp. 1–13. DOI: https://doi.org/10.3390/su11113130.

Högholm, K., (2016) Bidder's Gain in Public M&A Transactions: Does Size Matter? *International Journal of Economics and Finance*, 85, p. 1. DOI: https://doi.org/10.5539/ijef.v8n5p1.

Hohl, P., Klünder, J., van Bennekum, A., Lockard, R., Gifford, J., Münch, J., Stupperich, M. and Schneider, K., (2018) Back to the future: origins and directions of the "Agile Manifesto"—views of the originators. *Journal of Software Engineering Research and Development*, 61. DOI: https://doi.org/10.1186/s40411-018-0059-z.

Holbeche, L., (2019) Designing sustainably agile and resilient organizations. *Systems Research and Behavioral Science*, 365, pp. 668–677. DOI: https://doi.org/10.1002/sres.2624.

Hromei, A.-S., (2013) Reasons for Mergers and their Impact on Companies. *SEA—Practical Application of Science*, I01, pp. 82–88. Available at: https://doaj.org/article/97cdfa26993b44ffb08562f083a18f68 [Accessed 17 Sept. 2020].

Huang, Z., Zhu, H.S. and Brass, D.J., (2017) Cross-border acquisitions and the asymmetric effect of power distance value difference on long-term post-acquisition performance. *Strategic Management Journal*, 384, pp. 972–991. DOI: https://doi.org/10.1002/smj.2530.

Hurta, H., Jazouli, A., Koplyay, T. and Motaghi, H., (2017) MERGERS AND ACQUISITIONS FROM THE PERSPECTIVE OF PROJECT MANAGEMENT. *Polish Journal of Management Studies*, 152, pp. 100–114. DOI: https://doi.org/10.17512/pjms.2017.15.2.10

www.imaa-institute.org. (n.d.), *IMAA*. [online] Available at: https://imaa-institute.org/mergers-and-acquisitions-statistics/ [Accessed 15 Dec. 2020].

Jansen, S.A., (2016) *Mergers & Acquisitions*. 6th ed. Wiesbaden: Springer Gabler. DOI: https://doi.org/10.1007/978-3-8349-4772-7.

Joshi, M., Sanchez, C. and Mudde, P., (2020) Improving the M&A success rate: identity may be the key. *Journal of Business Strategy*, 411, pp. 50–57. DOI: https://doi.org/10.1108/JBS-08-2017-0115.

Junni, P., Sarala, R.M., Tarba, S.Y. and Weber, Y., (2015) The Role of Strategic Agility in Acquisitions. *British Journal of Management*, 264, pp. 596–616. DOI: https://doi.org/10.1111/1467-8551.12115.

Kaushik, V. and Walsh, C.A., (2019) Pragmatism as a research paradigm and its implications for Social Work research. *Social Sciences*, 89. DOI: https://doi.org/10.3390/socsci8090255.

Kim, T. and Donaldson, T., (2018) Rethinking Right: Moral Epistemology in Management Research. *Journal of Business Ethics*, 1481, pp. 5–20. DOI: https://doi.org/10.1007/s10551-015-3009-2.

Koi-Akrofi, G.Y., (2016) Mergers and Acquisitions Failure Rates and Perspectives On Why They Fail. *International Journal of Innovation and Applied Studies*, [online] 171, pp. 150–158. Available at: http://search.proquest.com.ezproxy.saintleo.edu/docview/1807743919?accountid=4870. [Accessed 12 Oct. 2020].

Kroon, D.P. and Noorderhaven, N.G., (2018) The Role of Occupational Identification During Post-Merger Integration. *Group and Organization Management*, 432, pp. 207–244. DOI: https://doi.org/10.1177/1059601116666168.

Lakshman, C., (2011) CULTURAL INTEGRATION IN M&A: A KNOWLEDGE-BASED APPROACH. *Human Resource Management*, 451, pp. 127–145. DOI: https://doi.org/10.1002/hrm.20447

Laloux, F., (2016) *Reinventing Organizations visuell*. 1st Ed. Munich: Vahlen. DOI: https://doi.org/10.15358/9783800652860.

Larsson, R. and Finkelstein, S., (1999) Integrating Strategic, Organizational, and Human Resource Perspectives on Mergers and Acquisitions: A Case Survey of Synergy Realization. *Organization Science*, 101, pp. 1–26. Available at: https://www.jstor.org/stable/2640385. [Accessed 29 Oct. 2020].

Lauser, B., (2010) Post-merger integration and change processes from a complexity perspective. *Baltic Journal of Management*, 51, pp. 6–27. DOI: https://doi.org/10.1108/17465261011016531.

Lee Marks, M., Mirvis, P. and Ashkenas, R., (2014) Making the Most of Culture Clash in M&A. *Leader to Leader*, 201471, pp. 45–53. DOI: https://doi.org/10.1002/ltl.20113.

MacIntosh, R. and O'Gorman, K.D., (2015) *Research Methods for Business Research Methods for Business*. 2nd Ed. Goodfellow Publishers Ltd: Wolvercote.

Maire, S. and Collerette, P., (2011) International post-merger integration: Lessons from an integration project in the private banking sector. *International Journal of Project Management*, [online] 293, pp. 279–294. Available at: https://doi.org/10.1016/j.ijproman.2010.03.001.

Majid, M.A.A., Othman, M., Mohamad, S.F., Lim, S.A.H. and Yusof, A., (2017) Piloting for Interviews in Qualitative Research: Operationalization and Lessons Learnt. *International Journal of Academic Research in Business and Social Sciences*, 74, pp. 1073–1080. DOI: https://doi.org/10.6007/ijarbss/v7-i4/2916

Martela, F., (2015) Fallible Inquiry with Ethical Ends-in-View: A Pragmatist Philosophy of Science for Organizational Research. *Organization Studies*, 364, pp. 537–563. DOI: https://doi.org/10.1177/0170840614559257

Meckl, R. and Röhrle, F., (2016) Do M&A deals create or destroy value? A meta-analysis. *European Journal of Business and Economics*, 112. DOI: https://doi.org/10.12955/ejbe.v11i2.890

Mercer, J., (2007) The challenges of insider research in educational institutions: wielding a double-edged sword and resolving delicate dilemmas. *Oxford Review of Education*, 331, pp. 1–17. DOI: https://doi.org/10.1080/03054980601094651

Mero-Jaffe, I., (2011) 'Is that what I Said?' Interview Transcript Approval by Participants: An Aspect of Ethics in Qualitative Research. *International Journal of Qualitative Methods*, 103, pp. 231–247. DOI: https://doi.org/10.1177/160940691101000304

Meynerts-Stiller, K., and Rohloff, C. (2019) *Post-Merger Management*. Emerald Publishing Limited. DOI: https://doi.org/10.1108/978-1-83867-451-920191001

Mikkelsen, M.F., (2016) How to cope with complexity [online] Available at: http://www.novateam.dk/PDF/IRIS2016_paper_20.pdf. [Accessed 19 Oct. 2020].

Moeller, S. and Brady, C., (2014) *Intelligent M&A*. 2nd ed. John Wiley and Sons, Ltd. DOI: https://doi.org/10.1002/9781118764220

Nazarian, M., (2017) Global Mergers and Acquisitions Analysis : Impact of Firm Size on Deal Success. pp. 1–24. Available at: http://www.etd.ceu.edu/2017/nazarian_maryna.pdf [Accessed 03 Oct. 2020].

Nguyen, C.A., (2013) Factors of Success and Failure in Mergers and Acquisitions. *Golden Gate University, ProQuest Dissertations Publishing*, [online] pp. 1–123. Available at: https://search.proquest.com/docview/1459823362?pq-origsite=summon&https://search.proquest.com/pqdtglobal/shibbolethlogin. [Accessed 23 Oct. 2020].

Patel, K., (2019) *Agile M&A*. Agile M&A Inc. Lightning Source Inc.: La Vergne

Patel, R., (2012) Applying Project Management Approaches To Achieve Value Creation In Post—Acquisition Integration. *The ISM Journal of International Business*, 14, pp. 1–30. Available at: http://connection.ebscohost.com/c/articles/90519438/applying-project-management-approaches-achieve-value-creation-post-acquisition-integration. [Accessed 03 Dec. 2020].

Patel, S., (2018) A Study towards the Influencing Factors of Leadership Styles and Impact on Employee Performance: An Empirical Study of Banking Sector. 0804, pp. 108–112. Available at: https://www.academia.edu/37452847/A_Study_towards_the_Influencing_Factors_of_Leadership_Styles_and_Impact_on_Employee_Performance_An_Empirical_Study_of_Banking_Sector. [Accessed 14 Dec. 2020].

Perry, J.S. and Herd, T.J., (2004) Reducing M&A risk through improved due diligence. *Strategy & Leadership*, 322, pp. 12–19. DOI: https://doi.org/10.1108/10878570410525089

Poveda-Bautista, R., Diego-Mas, J.A. and Leon-Medina, D., (2018) Measuring the Project Management Complexity: The Case of Information Technology Projects. *Complexity*, 2018 May. DOI: https://doi.org/10.1155/2018/6058480

Preußig, J., (2018) *Agiles Projektmanagement – Agilität und Scrum im klassischen Projektumfeld*. Haufe. DOI: https://doi.org/10.34157/9783648105917

Project Management Institute, (2017) *PMBOK GUIDE. A Guide to the Project Management Body of Knowledge (PMBOK® Guide)—Sixth Edition*. Newtown Square, Pa.: Project Management Institute.

Puik, E. and Ceglarek, D., (2015) The Quality of a Design will not Exceed the Knowledge of its Designer; An Analysis Based on Axiomatic Information and the Cynefin Framework. *Procedia CIRP*, [online] 34, pp. 19–24. Available at: https://doi.org/10.1016/j.procir.2015.07.040.

PWC (2016) Mergers & Acquisitions. *Price Waterhouse Coopers Report 06/2016*, Available at: https://www.pwc.nl/nl/assets/documents/pwc-mergers-acquisitions.pdf [Accessed 20 Oct. 2020].

PWC (2020) Evolving with agility: PwC's 2020 M&A Integration Survey. Available at: https://www.pwc.com/us/en/services/deals/library/ma-integration-survey.html [Accessed 11 Oct. 2020].

Rasnacis, A. and Berzisa, S., (2016) Method for Adaptation and Implementation of Agile Project Management Methodology. *Procedia Computer Science*, 104, pp. 43–50. DOI: https://doi.org/10.1016/j.procs.2017.01.055

Rebner, S. and Yeganeh, B., (2019) Mindful Mergers & Acquisitions. *OD Practitioner*, [online] 511, pp. 11–16. Available at: https://static1.squarespace.com/static/5ea39a89c76f373be702d49a/t/5ea4b2cb00047c5743c20cf9/1587851980083/OD+Review-vol51+no1+-+Rebner+%26+Yeganeh.pdf [Accessed 18 Oct. 2020].

Rowley, J., (2012) Conducting research interviews. *Management Research Review*, 353–4, pp. 260–271. DOI: https://doi.org/10.1108/01409171211210154.

Rozen-Bakher, Z., (2018) Labour productivity in M&As: industry sector vs. services sector. *Service Industries Journal*, 3815–16, pp. 1043–1066. DOI: https://doi.org/10.1080/02642069.2017.1397136.

Rubin, H. and Rubin, I., (2012) *Qualitative Interviewing (2nd ed.): The Art of Hearing Data. Qualitative Interviewing (2nd ed.): The Art of Hearing Data.* DOI: https://doi.org/10.4135/9781452226651.

Ruwhiu, D. and Cone, M., (2010) Advancing a pragmatist epistemology in organisational research. *Qualitative Research in Organizations and Management: An International Journal*, 52, pp. 108–126. DOI: https://doi.org/10.1108/17465641011068884

Saldana, J., (2009) *The Coding Manual for Qualitative Researchers.* London: SAGE Publications Ltd. Available at: https://www.academia.edu/11310253/The_coding_manual_for_qualitative_researchers [Accessed 12 Dec. 2020].

Salmons, J., (2015) Designing and Conducting Research with Online Interviews. In: *Cases in Online Interview Research.* DOI: https://doi.org/10.4135/9781506335155.n1.

Sanchez, O.P., Terlizzi, M.A. and de Moraes, H.R. de O.C., (2017) Cost and time project management success factors for information systems development projects. *International Journal of Project Management*, 358, pp. 1608–1626. DOI: https://doi.org/10.1016/j.ijproman.2017.09.007.

Saunders, M., Lewis, P. and Thornhill, A., (2016) Formulating the research design. *Research Methods for Business Students.* New York: Pearson Education Limited.

Saunders, M., Lewis, P. and Thornhill, A., (2019) *Research methods for business students, 8th edition.* New York: Pearson Education Limited.

Schein, E.H., (2004) *Organizational Culture and Leadership*, Third Edition. San Francisco: Jossey-Bass.

Schirl-Boeck, I. and Nachgabauer, A., (2019) Managing surprises and turbulences in projects: Extending the Cynefin framework. Available at: https://www.researchgate.net/publication/334251231 [Accessed 03 Oct. 2020].

Schönreiter, I.M., (2018) Methodologies for process harmonization in the post-merger integration phase: A literature review. *Business Process Management Journal*, 242, pp. 330–356. DOI: https://doi.org/10.1108/BPMJ-07-2016-0141.

Schwaber, K. and Sutherland, J., (2017) The Scrum Guide: The Definitive The Rules of the Game. *Scrum.Org and Scrum Inc*, [online] November, p.19. Available at: http://www.scrumguides.org/docs/scrumguide/v1/Scrum-Guide-US.pdf. [Accessed 15 Oct. 2020].

Sharma, M., (2016) Cross Border Mergers and Acquisitions and The Exchange Rate: A Literature Review. *Journal of International Economics (0976–0792)*, [online] 72, pp. 23–34. Available at: https://www.semanticscholar.org/paper/CROSS-BORDER-MERGERS-AND-ACQUISITIONS-AND-THE-RATE-Sharma/9903f57e16d0fbb5b6165e9e53f37fa65386e6b8. [Accessed 04 Oct. 2020].

Sherman, A., (2018) *Mergers & Acquisitions from A to Z*. 4th ed. Nashville: Harpercollins Focus.

Shi, H.L. and Wang, Y.M., (2020) A Merger and Acquisition Matching Method That Considers Irrational Behavior from a Performance Perspective. *IEEE Access*, 8, pp. 45726–45737. DOI: https://doi.org/10.1109/ACCESS.2020.2976608.

Sil, R., (2008) Simplifying Pragmatism : From Social Theory to Problem-driven Eclecticism. pp. 648–652. Available at: https://www.academia.edu/1634598/Simplifying_Pragmatism_From_Social_Theory_to_Problem_Driven_Eclecticism [Accessed 04 Oct. 2020].

Smaling, A., (1994) The pragmatic dimension—Paradigmatic and pragmatic aspects of choosing a qualitative or quantitative method. *Quality & Quantity*, 283, pp. 233–249. DOI: https://doi.org/10.1007/BF01098942.

Smeets, V., Ierulli, K. and Gibbs, M., (2016) An Empirical Analysis of Post-Merger Organizational Integration. *Scandinavian Journal of Economics*, 1183, pp. 463–493. DOI: https://doi.org/10.1111/sjoe.12161.

Smith, P., da Cunha, J.V., Giangreco, A., Vasilaki, A. and Carugati, A., (2013) The threat of dis-identification for HR practices: An ethnographic study of a merger. *European Management Journal*, [online] 313, pp. 308–321. Available at: https://doi.org/10.1016/j.emj.2012.07.004.

Snowden, D.J. and Boone, M.E., (2007) BGS Session 5 : *Harvard Business Review*, [online] 74, pp. 1–6. Available at: https://www.researchgate.net/publication/5689229_A_Leader%27s_Framework_for_Decision_Making [Accessed 07 Nov. 2020].

Sohi, A.J., Hertogh, M., Bosch-Rekveldt, M. and Blom, R., (2016) Does Lean & Agile Project Management Help Coping with Project Complexity? *Procedia—Social and Behavioral Sciences*, [online] 226July, pp. 252–259. Available at: https://doi.org/10.1016/j.sbspro.2016.06.186.

Spoor, J.R. and Chu, M.T., (2018) The Role of Social Identity and Communities of Practice in Mergers and Acquisitions. *Group and Organization Management*, 434, pp. 623–647. DOI: https://doi.org/10.1177/1059601117703266.

Stacey, R.D., (2007) *Strategic Management and Organisational Dynamics*. 5th ed. Harlow: Pearson.

Stahl, G.K., Larsson, R., Kremershof, I. and Sitkin, S.B., (2011) Trust dynamics in acquisitions: A case survey. *Human Resource Management*, 505, pp. 575–603. DOI: https://doi.org/10.1108/S1479-361X(2010)0000009006.

Stankiewicz-Mróz, A., (2015) Approach to the Issues of Leadership in the Processes of Companies' Acquisitions. *Procedia Manufacturing*, 3Ahfe, pp. 793–798. DOI: https://doi.org/10.1016/j.promfg.2015.07.332.

Steigenberger, N., (2017) The Challenge of Integration: A Review of the M&A Integration Literature. *International Journal of Management Reviews*, 194, pp. 408–431. DOI: https://doi.org/10.1111/ijmr.12099

Stone, E.J., Times, A. and Clemente, Ó.M.N., (2000) Protecting Yourself from M & A Disasters. pp. 13–16. DOI: https://doi.org/10.1002/(SICI)1097-0053(200001/02)11:2<13::AID-JCAF4>3.0.CO;2-1.

Taguchi, N., (2018) Description and explanation of pragmatic development: Quantitative, qualitative, and mixed methods research. *System*, [online] 75, pp. 23–32. Available at: https://doi.org/10.1016/j.system.2018.03.010.

Tarba, S. and Weber, Y., (2011) Exploring integration approach in related mergers: Post-merger integration in the high-tech industry. *International Journal of Organizational Analysis*, 193, pp. 202–221. DOI: https://doi.org/10.1108/19348831111149178.

Tetenbaum, T.J., (1999) Seven key practices. *Organizational Dynamics*, 282, pp. 22–36. DOI: https://doi.org/10.1016/s0090-2616(00)80014-5

Torraco, R.J., (2016) Writing Integrative Reviews of the Literature. *International Journal of Adult Vocational Education and Technology*, 73, pp. 62–70. DOI: https://doi.org/10.4018/IJAVET.2016070106

Trichterborn, A., Knyphausen-Aufseß, D. and Schweizer, L., (2015) HOW TO IMPROVE ACQUISITION PERFORMANCE: THE ROLE OF A DEDICATED M&A FUNCTION, M&A LEARNING PROCESS, AND M&A CAPABILITY. *Strategic Management Journal*, 37 February 2015, pp. 763–773. DOI: https://doi.org/10.1002/smj.2364

Venzin, M., Vizzaccaro, M. and Rutschmann, F., (2018) Negotiation and Deal Closing. *Making Mergers and Acquisitions Work*. Bingley: Emerald.

Waldman, D.A. and Javidan, M., (2009) Alternative forms of charismatic leadership in the integration of mergers and acquisitions. *Leadership Quarterly*, [online] 202, pp. 130–142. Available at: https://doi.org/10.1016/j.leaqua.2009.01.008.

Wojatzki, M., Mohammad, S.M., Zesch, T. and Kiritchenko, S., (2019) Quantifying qualitative data for understanding controversial issues. *LREC 2018—11th International Conference on Language Resources and Evaluation*, pp. 1405–1418. DOI: https://doi.org/10.17185/duepublico/46420.

Yeganeh, B., (2016) Mindfulness as a Disruptive Approach to Leader Development. *Od Practitioner*, 481, pp. 26–31. Availabe at: https://static1.squarespace.com/static/5ea39a89c76f373be702d49a/t/5ea4b343dd54754687278556/1587852099262/ODP-V48%2CNo1-Yeganeh+and+Good.pdf [Accessed 07 Nov. 2020].

Yu, G.J., Park, M. and Hong, K.H., (2020) A strategy perspective on total quality management. *Total Quality Management and Business Excellence*, 311–2, pp. 68–81. DOI: https://doi.org/10.1080/14783363.2017.1412256

Zarb, B.J. and Noth, C., (2012) Do Integration Strategies and Supply Chain Relationships Play a Role in the Success or Failure of Mergers and Acquisitions? *International Journal of Business & Economics Perspectives*, [online] 71, pp. 68–81. Available at: https://works.bepress.com/bert_j_zarb/5/ [Accessed 19 Oct. 2020].

Zhang, J., Ahammad, M.F., Tarba, S., Cooper, C.L., Glaister, K.W. and Wang, J., (2015) The effect of leadership style on talent retention during Merger and Acquisition integration: evidence from China. *International Journal of Human Resource Management*, 267, pp. 1021–1050. DOI: https://doi.org/10.1080/09585192.2014.908316.

Zhou, C., Xie, J. and Wang, Q., (2016) Failure to Complete Cross-Border M&As: 'to' vs. 'from' Emerging Markets. *Journal of International Business Studies*, 479, pp. 1077–1105. DOI: https://doi.org/10.1057/s41267-016-0027-y.

The manufacturer's authorised representative in the EU is Springer Nature Customer Service Centre GmbH, Europaplatz 3, 69115 Heidelberg, Germany. If you have any concerns regarding our products, please contact ProductSafety@springernature.com

Printed and bound by CPI Group (UK) Ltd, Croydon, CR0 4YY
30/09/2026
02225468-0001